T0326298

THE HISTORY AND MECHANISM
OF THE
EXCHANGE EQUALISATION ACCOUNT

THE
HISTORY AND MECHANISM
OF THE
EXCHANGE EQUALISATION
ACCOUNT

by

LEONARD WAIGHT

Χρώμεθα γὰρ πολιτείᾳ οὐ ζηλούσῃ τοὺς τῶν πέλας νόμους,
παράδειγμα δὲ μᾶλλον αὐτοὶ ὄντες τισὶν ἢ μιμούμενοι ἑτέρους.
PERICLES, *Thucydides* II. 37

*Our form of government does not enter into rivalry with
the institutions of others. We do not copy our neighbours,
but are an example to them.*

JOWETT

CAMBRIDGE
AT THE UNIVERSITY PRESS
1939

CAMBRIDGE
UNIVERSITY PRESS

University Printing House, Cambridge CB2 8BS, United Kingdom

Cambridge University Press is part of the University of Cambridge.

It furthers the University's mission by disseminating knowledge in the pursuit of
education, learning and research at the highest international levels of excellence.

www.cambridge.org
Information on this title: www.cambridge.org/9781316611715

© Cambridge University Press 1939

First published 1939
First paperback edition 2016

A catalogue record for this publication is available from the British Library

ISBN 978-1-316-61171-5 Paperback

To

R. M. W.

FOREWORD

MR LEONARD WAIGHT's study of the history and method of operation of the Exchange Equalisation Fund is, so far as I know, the first one to be published. It therefore fills a need which has been experienced, not only by students of the financial machine of this country, but by a wider circle of people who are generally interested in current economic affairs. The introductory chapters dealing with matters of recent history and everyday practice, such as the money market, foreign exchange business and the Bank of England return, will already be familiar both to students and those who have a practical acquaintance with the City. For the intelligent layman the volume stands complete in itself without his having to go elsewhere for an introduction to cognate subjects.

The first study of the Exchange Equalisation Fund made by Professor Noel Hall in 1935 (*The Exchange Equalisation Account*, Macmillan and Co. Ltd.) revealed consequences in the operation of the Fund which were not suspected by the general public and were perhaps only vaguely realised by those to whom the Fund owed its existence when it was conceived and born in the critical period of 1931–32. Mr Waight will be the first to acknowledge that the genesis of the present volume is in Professor Hall's illuminating study, which is now carried a stage further, for the author has added from his own practical acquaintance with the foreign exchange market, comments and descriptions of recent events down to the end of 1938.

There are two aspects of Mr Waight's study which must be mentioned. In his description of methods practised in the foreign exchange market, in which the Exchange Equalisation Fund plays so large a role, and in his comments on the effects which such transactions have on the money market, Mr Waight is drawing on practical experience. Such comments may form the subject of discussion among experts and interpretations from the available data of common experience are of course proper subjects for technical controversy, but they are based upon wide common knowledge. When however the author makes deductions from such figures as are available, as for instance of the state of the Fund at any moment, the magnitude of gold movements and hoards, etc., he has of course had to use only the incomplete figures available to the public. This side of his study is necessarily therefore conjectural, since outside the Treasury and the Bank of England the full figures for arriving at accurate results are not available. This then is a field of inference and not of fact or experience. To put it more simply: certain of Mr Waight's conclusions contained for instance in the table facing p. 82 are intelligent guesswork, founded upon the incomplete data available to any student to make another guess. It is necessary to sound this warning lest more should be read into these tables and relevant comments than the author intends. The historian may well find hereafter that much in this field of Mr Waight's book will need revision in the light of further information. He will nevertheless have had the advantage of understanding how the situation appeared to contemporaries. He will moreover have the inestimable convenience of finding in one volume (Appendices A–F) a corpus of the legislative documents which affect the subject.

No further introduction seems necessary save to add that this, Mr Waight's first volume, has received the commendation of Professor Noel Hall himself as well as of other technicians who have had the advantage of seeing it in draft form.

FRANCIS RODD

January 1939

CONTENTS

PART III

xi

* This four tables are available for download from www.cambridge.org/9781316611715

PREFACE

On 15 April 1932 the House of Commons debated the question of the Exchange Equalisation Account. In the course of the debate Sir A. M. Samuel (now Lord Mancroft) said:

I...urge that...we should explain to the people the meaning of our exchange policy, how it operates and what we shall try to make it do.

In the syllabus of the Associate Examination of the Institute of Bankers, under the heading of "Foreign Exchange", it states that questions may be set on

...Exchange Equalisation Accounts in theory and practice and their connection with and effects on the domestic credit and banking systems; managed currency systems and exchanges; special features of exchanges under the events of the last two decades, with special reference to the past few years.

The above quotations provide the motive for this book.

There are many excellent books on Foreign Exchange written before the exchange fund regime was inaugurated. Some of the theories expounded therein are vitally compromised if not rendered obsolete by the new technique developed in this and other countries since 1931. Those which have been revised to include modern practice deal very inadequately with the subject and give little assistance to the student or general reader. There is also the recognised classic, *Exchange Equalisation Account*, by Professor N. F. Hall, which no student can afford to overlook. It is an outline and an examination of the policy of the Exchange Equalisation Account up to 1935 and is primarily intended for the advanced student or the specialist. Thus, there appears to be a need for a text-book dealing with the *modus operandi* of the Exchange Equalisation Account and its "effects on the domestic credit and banking system".

This work is not offered as an exhaustive study of the history of the Exchange Equalisation Account. The time has not yet come for that to be undertaken. The aim has been to select the principal phases and events in its history and use them to illustrate in a comprehensive way the evolutionary character of the mechanism employed.

The elementary nature of the work must be stressed; nevertheless, in the presentation of the facts and assumptions on a matter which bristles with technicalities it has been found impossible to exclude the use of many technical terms and phrases. Some atonement has been made by the provision of a glossary of the more important terms used.

In asking for the usual tolerance for any errors of fact or questionable assumptions which may have been made, I must plead in mitigation the secrecy of official operations, which leave the area of exact knowledge on the subject very much circumscribed.

Many of the chapters of this book were already in type when the Bank of England announced the transfer of £200 millions in gold to the Exchange Equalisation Account, and, later, the Currency and Bank Notes Act 1939 was passed.

These important changes came too late to permit the necessary amendments to the text of this book. Instead, footnotes have been inserted where the matter has been compromised by these changes, discussion on which will be found in the Addenda on p. 143.

I wish to acknowledge my indebtedness to the Editor of the *Financial Times* for permission to reproduce in Chapter 10 an article written by me on the sterling gold price and published in that journal on 15 August 1938.

Finally, I must express my appreciation and thanks to my colleague, Mr S. Douglas Rae, for much valuable help in checking the statistical material.

LEONARD WAIGHT

April 1939

PART I

CHAPTER 1

O N 21 SEPTEMBER 1931 the gold bullion standard operated by Britain since 1925 was suspended. In April 1932 the Exchange Equalisation Account was set up and has remained in force ever since. In order that we may properly understand the connection between these events we must go back a little and enquire into the circumstances which led up to them.

The gold standard suspension was an act of supreme importance in Britain's financial history and one that has had far-reaching repercussions not only in this country but throughout the world. In other countries it gave rise to much bewilderment, bitterness and nervousness. If the foundations of the citadel of financial probity were unsound and the structure about to tumble, other centres could not remain for long unaffected.

At that time there was considerable controversy concerning the necessity for such a drastic step and many criticisms from abroad were erroneously based on the assumption that it was a Machiavellian plot to capture world trade. The passing of time enables a better perspective to be drawn, and with it an understanding of those deep-seated forces which made the suspension inevitable. It is necessary for our purpose to make a rapid review of those forces.

The war of 1914–18, with all its terrific strain on the financial structure of this country, was maintained without suspending the gold standard *de jure*. The dollar-sterling ratio was pegged at just under the gold standard parity. Britain was able to ensure this rate, firstly, by borrowing to finance war purchases instead of selling sterling and buying dollars; secondly, by mobilising British holdings of American securities; and finally, when

America entered the war as an associate, by United States Government loans. In effect the gold standard, internally and externally, was inoperative.

After the war the pound sterling was left to find its own level and it fluctuated considerably. In 1925 the pound was put on its pre-war gold basis and with it the pre-war dollar-sterling ratio. The unwisdom of that step was not generally recognised at the time, though there were a few far-seeing persons who protested vigorously against the decision. The fact that Britain was still a large creditor nation had a great bearing on the decision. If the pound had been devalued the nation's income from foreign investments would have been correspondingly reduced. The authorities did not overlook the fact that by restoring the pound to its pre-war parity with the dollar some over-valuation of the pound would result. But they had reason to believe that the initial over-valuation would be corrected by the intensive reorganisation—in those days it was called rationalisation—of industry which was in progress at that time. In the event, these hopes were not fulfilled. The over-valuation of the pound—which some economists estimated as something of the order of 15%—persisted because it was found impossible to reduce wages, taxes, overheads and other fundamental costs beyond a certain point. This rigidity of the cost structure was not comprehended sufficiently until some time after the restoration of the pound.

One of the fundamental differences between the pre-war and post-war conditions was in regard to the nature of the basis of the London Money Market. London's pre-war financial supremacy was based on three main factors. It was an international lender with unsurpassed knowledge; it operated the gold standard with a freedom which was unique, and it had developed a bill market which held the admiration of the world. The sterling bill was backed up by the unrivalled facilities of the acceptance and discount market in London and the high traditions and integrity of the names forming that market. London was the acceptance banker for the world, and the bill of exchange was the instrument. That instrument is an ideal one because, being based on wanted goods or services the bill of exchange is self-liquidating. The short-loan fund* of the London financial market was vitalised by the bill of exchange; by its use it combined in a high degree the greatest safety consistent with the greatest liquidity.

The destruction by the war of a large part of Britain's international trade and the financing of international trade, as well as the piling up of a huge internal and external debt occasioned by the war, considerably reduced the volume of the bills of exchange in London. Their place was taken by Treasury Bills. A large part of the enormous legacy debt of the war was unfunded short-term debt, of which a considerable part was in the form of Treasury Bills. We shall have occasion in later chapters to refer to the great part which the Treasury Bill has had in the post-war history of the London Money Market, especially in regard to the Exchange Equalisation Account. Here we are concerned with it as the instrument which has largely replaced the bill of exchange. The Treasury Bill converted London's position of international acceptance banker to international deposit banker. London arrived at that position after the return to the gold standard in 1925. So long as sterling was not interchangeable with gold there were definite risks attached to the holding of that currency by foreigners. They could not be sure what the exchange rate would be when they wished to repatriate their money. The attachment of sterling to gold removed that risk, and foreign funds poured into London to be employed in what was regarded as the safest short-term security in the world —the British Treasury Bill.

It was simple enough and very attractive for the foreigners to remit funds to London where they could be left on deposit with the banks and, more important, could be withdrawn at will without capital loss. That was possible because Britain, having returned to the gold standard, had rendered the pound sterling interchangeable with gold. The London banks which received their deposits would normally employ their funds or a proportion of them in the short-loan market, the basis of which was the

* For definitions of technical terms used in the work see Glossary on p. 182.

bill of exchange, but as there were insufficient bills available, the banks sought another outlet, which was the British Treasury Bill.

Britain's return to the gold standard in 1925 was followed by many other countries which had suspended or rendered it inoperative on the outbreak of war. Some of them adopted what is known as the gold exchange standard, which means in simple language that the Central Bank of the country adopting the standard was authorised to hold gold and/or gold standard currencies as a basis for the note circulation. As London had acquired a reputation for operating the gold standard without any restrictions on the withdrawal of gold*—a feature that was not common to all gold standard operating countries—it was chosen by many countries as the centre in which the currency assets of the Central Banks concerned should be held. Sterling held on deposit in London could be exchanged for gold at any time. Deposits provide an income, gold does not.

London became a magnet for funds from all over the world, and, if the owners of those funds were content to leave them here, bankers who were the recipients of them were hard put to it to find outlets. It was perhaps not unnatural that some part of those funds was employed in more remunerative ways than by the purchase of Treasury Bills. In a post-war Europe needing capital reconstruction, and other parts of the world needing capital of which they had been starved during the war years, there were profitable or what seemed to be profitable outlets for employment of money. London was quick to resume its former role as a supplier of capital, and considerable amounts were so exported. In view of subsequent events to which we shall refer later, the export of that capital was, in some cases, unwise. London was borrowing on short term and lending on long term. The export of capital on such a scale and the growing adverse balance of trade might have easily brought about the breakdown of the gold standard much sooner than 1931 but for other factors which served to mask the real position. We must consider those factors.

* Cf. p. 7.

⟨ 4 ⟩

America made great efforts during the war and especially in the years just after the war to replace Britain as the world's supplier of capital. She embarked on a policy of foreign lending on a great scale to countries all over the world. In the years from 1923 to 1929 Continental Europe was able to borrow many millions of dollars from America; Germany in particular borrowed more from America and Britain than it paid in reparations. There was a two-way flow of funds. The westward flow, creating buyers of dollars, had its origin in the large adverse trade balance between Europe and America. The latter country sold more products than it bought from Europe. In addition large amounts of dollars were wanted by ·Europe for payment of the semi-annual instalments on war debt account. The eastward flow, creating sellers of dollars, had its origin in the large amount of loans made by America to many European countries. The westward and eastward flow did not exactly balance; the difference was made up by shipments of gold to America where, in the post-war years, huge quantities were amassed. Without the eastward flow Britain would have had great difficulty in maintaining its currency on a gold basis.

All this time large sums of money were being transferred on War Debt account. Britain was receiving payments from France, Italy and others, and America was receiving larger sums from all the Allies. From 1923 to 1932 Britain paid to America £400 millions on War Debt account. There were therefore huge displacements of funds in and out of Britain, on commercial as well as Government account, constituting a perilous position because a balance could be maintained only so long as *all* those movements of capital continued to be made. The cessation of one would bring about a collapse of the whole structure. That in fact happened.

Internally, the position of Britain steadily deteriorated. There was considerable labour unrest; prolonged strikes and growing unemployment and other signs of economic disorder which were aggravated by the return to gold. The British price level was much above the world level, and in consequence export markets were steadily lost to us. Employers found that beyond

⟨ 5 ⟩

a certain point the wage structure was too rigid to be compressed further. Production was therefore curtailed. Meanwhile Britain had become a free trade island in a world of protected markets. Not only were goods of other countries imported in increasing quantities but the proceeds, i.e. pounds sterling, were offered against other currencies requiring ultimately a settlement in gold. Thus the economic position of Britain was out of balance and a breakdown somewhere was only a question of time.

Perhaps the drying up of American loans to Europe started the long train of events, each more serious than the last, leading up to the culminating point of Britain's suspension of the gold standard. Cause and effect were hopelessly mixed. It may have been the French occupation of the Ruhr, or the general strike in Britain, or the Wall Street crash in America, or the Credit Anstalt crash in Austria which lighted the trail leading up to the Hoover moratorium and the greatest depression the modern world has known—a depression unique inasmuch as not one country in the whole world escaped its blight.

As for Britain, first there was the Macmillan Committee's report on finance and industry which drew attention to the vulnerability of the London Money Market, and then the May Committee's report which shouted to the world that we were living beyond our means and caused a wave of apprehension abroad which did not quite give way to panic. Britain, it was thought, would somehow muddle through again. The Bank of England obtained franc and dollar credits to a total of £50 millions, but they were not sufficient to stem the flow of gold. In addition, and for the same purpose, the Treasury obtained credits for £80 millions, but the loss of gold continued. The Labour Government gave way to a three-party Government which enforced a drastic cutting of expenditure, including the pay of Judges, Civil Servants and of the armed forces. The "mutiny" of Invergordon caused by inequalities in sailors' pay was the culminating incident, magnified by the Press, that convinced foreigners that their money in Britain was no longer safe. The funds lent by Britain on long term could not be recalled against the rapid withdrawal of the short-term funds borrowed. There ensued a run on the diminishing stock of gold of the Bank of England. In two months £200 millions of foreign-owned funds were withdrawn from the London market. At the end, the gold remaining with the Bank of England amounted to £130 millions, equal to the amount of the recently arranged credits of the Bank of England and Treasury. There was not enough cash available either in the large banks or in the Bank of England to meet the sight liabilities which were being hastily realised.

Britain had no option but to suspend the gold standard.

Much that has happened since has restored the pride and prestige which were so humbled on 21 September 1931. We have learned since what should have been apparent in 1925 when the decision was taken to restore the pre-war value of sterling, that even strong nations like Britain cannot participate in a four-years' world war without running up a bill of a size that effectively prevents a return to former conditions. In particular we have learned that London as a world financial centre has changed its essential characteristics. It is vulnerable to an extreme degree unless measures are designed and actively pursued in its defence. The needed design and action arrived in April 1932, and it was called the Exchange Equalisation Account.

CHAPTER 2

THE period between the suspension of the gold standard in September 1931 and the establishment of the Exchange Equalisation Account in April 1932 was a critical one. The pound sterling in terms of gold currencies fluctuated violently. In terms of the dollar the rate plunged to 3·25⅜ and in terms of the franc to 83⅛ as against the gold parities of $4·86⅔ and fr. 124 respectively. Later, when it was seen that resolute efforts were being made to balance the budget and to correct the adverse trade balance by the imposition of a tariff, confidence in the British currency returned. The violent oscillations of the exchange rates, largely caused by the operations of the currency speculator, were very disconcerting to importers and exporters, who were unable to find a firm base on which to make prices for their trading. This was inimical to a situation in which everything that was calculated to assist industry and employment in this country formed part of the declared policy for which the Government was returned to power by such an overwhelming majority.

In the early months of 1932 confidence in sterling returned with such force that unless steps had been taken to counteract the movement sterling would have been forced back to a level which would have deprived the economic and financial fabric of the advantages accruing from a proper valuation *vis-à-vis* foreign currencies and gold. This appreciation in the value of sterling continued although large purchases of dollars and francs were being made by the British Treasury and the Bank for the purpose of repaying the credits obtained from America and France referred to in the previous chapter. When it became known that these credits had been repaid, the movement was accentuated. All this was very flattering to this country, but it was inconvenient and even harmful, and something had to be done about it.

The Bank of England in its capacity as agent for the British

Treasury and as the institution called upon "to keep the financial structure on an even keel", within its limited scope, endeavoured to control the fluctuations of the pound in terms of other currencies. It operated in the market as buyer or seller of foreign currencies, with the object of reducing the fluctuations in range and frequency. It soon proved to be a task beyond its powers, for reasons of which we must here take note.

The Bank had definite statute limitations. The Gold Standard (Amendment) Act 1931* expressly relieved the Bank of England from the obligations laid upon it by the Gold Standard Act 1925† to sell gold at 77s. 10½d. per standard ounce, but the obligation to buy gold offered to it at the fixed price of 77s. 9d. per standard ounce remains. As the market price was at that time about 113s. per fine ounce the Bank could not hope to acquire any gold at its fixed price; so that it could not operate in the market as a buyer. As a seller the Bank was not free, since the gold holdings of the Issue Department constituted the cover for the repayment of the balance outstanding of the French and American credits‡ which had been contracted on a gold basis. If it obtained gold through the purchase of gold currencies, the transaction would eventually have to be expressed in the Bank of England's balance-sheet in terms of sterling, and as the currencies would have been acquired at varying prices the gold equivalent in terms of sterling would have been necessarily at varying prices too, importing undesirable complications of accountancy in the Bank's books. Moreover, the Issue Department of the Bank of England was not authorised to hold foreign currencies as part of its assets.§ The capital and other resources of the Bank of England being limited, any further purchases of foreign exchange were not possible without expanding the credit base unduly. It was felt that the main thing at that time was to prevent a rise in prices which, with an expanding credit base, might have led us into a spiral of inflation, of which we were all afraid, having become unanchored from an automatic exchange

* See Appendix C.　　　　† See Appendix A.　　　　‡ Cf. p. 6.
§ The ambiguity of the Currency and Bank Notes Act 1928 in this connection was removed by the Exchange Equalisation Account clauses of the Finance Act 1932, q.v. p. 166.

regulator. The abyss of inflation into which fell some Continental countries in the post-war years was remembered, and there is little doubt that the authorities at that time were haunted by this fear. These were the compelling reasons for the continuance of a high Bank Rate (although on other grounds perhaps illogical) and for the seeking of a solution to the formidable problem of devising an instrument which by its power and resources would draw the respect of speculators and possess the means and ability not only to control the external value of sterling but also to insulate the domestic credit structure.

It is permissible to claim that the solution decided upon was a masterpiece of British improvisation. The requirements were simple: a fund large enough to draw the respect of speculators, and authority to act, widely and secretly. Parliament granted the authority and provided the funds in the Finance Act of 1932.* Many Members of Parliament strongly objected to the operations of the Act and the results of those operations being withheld from Parliament until after the authority was terminated. Much of the newly created power would have been lost if the operations undertaken were made common knowledge. Such knowledge in the possession of world speculators could have enabled them to defeat the objects for which the authority and the public funds were granted. The possibility of large losses being made while carrying out authorised operations was made use of to support the objection to secrecy, and although that point of view is quite understandable, much of the criticism of this kind was based on incomplete knowledge of the essential requirements and of the technical conditions under which the authority would act. Subsequent statements made by the Chancellor of the Exchequer on Budget day have reassured Parliament. Little, if any, criticism of this nature now finds expression. Moreover, in 1937, five years after the authority was set up, the Chancellor of the Exchequer announced that the gold holdings henceforth would be given twice yearly but three months late, a concession much welcomed as being useful information without giving any benefit to speculators.

* For the relevant clauses of the Finance Act see Appendix D.

The Finance Act of 1932 authorised the setting up of an account to be known as the Exchange Equalisation Account (hereinafter referred to as E.E.A.). We shall consider in subsequent chapters to what extent it has justified its name.

Its objects were, in the words of Mr Neville Chamberlain,* the Chancellor of the Exchequer at that time, to

smooth out the variations in exchange caused by three sets of phenomena—firstly, the seasonal fluctuations; secondly, the operations of speculators, which increase those seasonal fluctuations, and other fluctuations, too; and, thirdly, this special flight of capital from other countries for the sake of finding a safer place to stop in for a time....

He continued:

...I would, however, emphasise once again that we are not proposing to utilise this fund for any other purpose than that which has been so often stated, namely, for removing undue fluctuations in the exchange value of the £.

For our purpose, explanatory remarks of greater length are here needed if we are to understand properly the purpose of the E.E.A.

We have seen that, since the suspension of the gold standard, sterling tumbled badly and then, after a period of considerable fluctuations, appreciably improved. Foreigners were not slow to comprehend the soundness of the remedial measures which were being carried through by the British people with such determination. In their estimation sterling had a greater value than was expressed in the current ratio of exchange with other currencies. Sterling's value should rise. There ensued a buying wave for pounds, not only speculatively in the hope of reselling later at a profit, but also for the purpose of employing those funds in this country in various ways, particularly in the purchase of shares of industrial companies which stood a good chance of benefiting by the imposition of a tariff. In addition, capital left the gold currency countries because it was feared that they too would have to follow Britain's example and leave

* Official Report, *Parliamentary Debates* (May 1933), 1038.

the gold standard. This type of money has been given such names as "fugitive capital", "hot money", etc.; the owners of it are very restless and do not hesitate to move it from one centre to another whenever they become nervous for its safety or see a chance of making a profit by exchanging into another currency. Whenever pounds flow in, inflationary forces are set up, and when they flow out, deflationary, which is worse unless they are offset in some way. This offsetting is one of the purposes of the E.E.A.

It was authorised to borrow from the Consolidated Fund up to a total of £150 millions, and to it was transferred the balance of £25 millions standing to the credit of the old Dollar Exchange Account. It was further authorised to reimburse to the Bank of England out of its resources a sum not exceeding £8 millions, being a loss* incurred by that institution in repaying the balance of credits obtained in France and America in August 1931. The E.E.A. therefore began operations as a Government department with capital assets amounting to £167 millions—a very formidable sum of money. In May 1933 the borrowing powers were increased by £200 millions, and in April 1937 by a further £200 millions, making a total fund of £567 millions.

The E.E.A. is controlled by the Treasury, while its actual operations are carried out by the Bank of England. The main operations take place in the Foreign Exchange Market, the Money Market and the Gold Market. The resources available have always enabled it to dominate all three markets, and indirectly it has a profound influence on the Stock Exchange. Before describing the mechanism of the E.E.A. and the effects of its operations on other markets, particularly the Money Market, it will be helpful if we explain the main principles which govern these operations.

The first principle is to counter any undue buying or selling of sterling not in any way connected with the normal purchases and sales on commercial account with which it is desired to interfere as little as possible. When, for example, sterling

---

* The total loss sustained in the repayment of the franc and dollar credits raised by the Treasury and Bank of England was £31 millions of which £23 millions was added to the National Debt.

is being bought not for the settlement of goods or services obtained in this country or for interest payments on money formerly borrowed or for any other normal procedure of this kind, but speculatively in anticipation of a profit on the purchase or because foreigners consider that their capital would be safer if converted into sterling, then it is the duty of the E.E.A. to sell sterling in the quantities required so that, supply and demand being equal, the exchange ratios of sterling with other currencies will not fluctuate to any great extent. Similarly, if for any reason other than normal sterling is subjected to pressure, that is, if it is being offered in large quantities, it is the duty of the E.E.A. to sell foreign currencies or gold and buy sterling, equating again, so far as possible, supply with demand, to maintain the exchange ratio. This has been described as "ironing out" fluctuations in the exchanges.

The second principle to be remembered is that from the point of view of the safety of the funds entrusted to the managers of the E.E.A. it is a fundamental obligation on them to exchange sterling, whenever they have to do so in accordance with the first principle, only for foreign currencies which can be exchanged for gold on demand. This is important for the primary reason just mentioned and because of subsequent changes in the characteristics of the E.E.A. into which we shall enquire later. Other countries followed Britain in suspending gold payments and operated a managed currency standard or what is more commonly known as a paper standard. The currencies of such countries were outside the sphere of operations of the E.E.A. because those currencies, if acquired, could not be automatically converted to gold. Britain can have no control whatever over the value of paper standard currencies, but as regards gold this country can ultimately fix a ratio of sterling to gold which it considers desirable.

There is a further reason why sterling should be exchanged only for gold. Foreign capital which sought refuge here will one day return to the country of origin, in which case the E.E.A. will be in a position to supply whichever currency is wanted if it has gold in its keeping. Gold gives safety as well as the maximum of utility from the point of view of the E.E.A.

The third principle is no less important. The acquisition of abnormal quantities of sterling by foreigners and the gold ultimately received in exchange for that sterling would normally expand the credit structure of this country; conversely, gold given in exchange for foreign-owned funds on repatriation would normally lead to a contraction of credit. But having vivid memories of the dire consequences which followed the sudden withdrawal of foreign capital from this country in 1931, the authorities have invented a means of neutralising such movements of capital. This principle, then, can be described as one of offsetting; offsetting an influx or efflux of foreign capital or insulating the domestic structure from irrelevant external influences.

We are now in a position to consider how these principles are applied, and that will be the subject of the next chapter.

CHAPTER 3

W E have seen that the E.E.A. was authorised originally to borrow up to £150 millions. Treasury Bills for that amount were issued to it out of the Consolidated Fund. Whenever it operates in the Foreign Exchange Market and needs funds, it disposes of some of its Treasury Bills in the money market up to the amount of pounds required above the £17 millions which it has had from the commencement, as was made clear in the last chapter. The operations of the E.E.A. impinge on at least two markets, first on the Foreign Exchange Market and then on the Money Market. It must borrow pounds from the second so as to be in a position to pay for the purchases of foreign currency which it has bought in the first market. The Gold Market and Stock Exchange are other spheres which at times bear the influence of the E.E.A.

A word or two here may not be out of place on the above-mentioned markets which provide the field of operations. Except for the Stock Exchange which is established in one building there is no physical market in the sense of its members meeting for the purpose of doing business in one building such as is the case with some commodity markets with which everyone is familiar.

The London Foreign Exchange Market comprises many banks—British, Dominion and Colonial, and foreign—each of which maintains a department to deal with foreign exchange business which is carried on with the constituents of that market through the medium of brokers who are in direct private line telephone contact with their principals—the banks. By telephone and cables the banks themselves are in close touch with money centres in other parts of the world, and by these contacts they can and do execute a large volume of business very rapidly which could not be achieved merely by representatives of banks and brokers meeting collectively in one place.

The Money Market* comprises all the banks mentioned in the above paragraph (in most cases other departments of the banks) and discount houses, bill brokers and running brokers. Contact is maintained by telephone and personal interview.

The Gold Market is a little different, in that the six gold brokers of the bullion market meet at the office of Messrs N. M. Rothschild and Sons, in St Swithin's Lane, each morning at 11 o'clock with the orders to purchase or sell gold on behalf of clients, principally banks, which the bullion brokers have received. The orders to buy and sell gold are pooled and are executed at a price arranged between all representatives who have regard to all the factors which go to establish the price. Those factors are many but they are outside the present theme.†

Paramount over all these markets is the Bank of England; its paramountcy is established not by enactment or autocratic usage but by the power of leverage its operations have on the Money Market and because it is the "lender of last resort", an expression which we shall explain later.

Let us now assume that pounds are being bought in large quantities and that the managers of the E.E.A. diagnose a flight of capital from France, for instance, and consider that it is their duty to intervene to prevent not only fluctuation of the exchange rate but also the influx of money expanding the credit base. Let us isolate one particular transaction out of the many and follow it through so that we may understand what is happening and why. This imaginary transaction is presumed to have taken place before France suspended the gold standard.

Monsieur Blank (to use a pseudonym to cover all those who think similarly) of Paris, considers that the economic and financial position in France is threatening the stability of the gold franc and, in consequence, he decides to transfer his liquid capital abroad. He instructs his banker, the "Paris Bank", to purchase for him say £1 million and to debit his current account with the cost in francs. The "Paris Bank" will either cover the transaction in the Paris market or will telephone to their corre-

* For a fuller description of the London Money Market see footnote on p. 39.
† They are explained in Chapter 10, p. 88.

spondents in London and purchase £1 million at an exchange rate of say fr. 75 to £1 from "London Bank" which in turn, finding that buyers of francs in the London market are scarce, decides to sell the fr. 75 millions which it has bought from Paris to the only firm buyer in the market, which at the moment is the Bank of England acting on behalf of the E.E.A. Two days later when the settlement of these transactions takes place the following items will be executed.* The presumed sequence is maintained.

Monsieur Blank will be credited with £1 million held in London on his behalf by "Paris Bank" and he will be debited with the cost in francs.

"Paris Bank" will credit "London Bank" with fr. 75 millions, and in their *nostro* account will debit "London Bank" with the counterpart £1 million. "London Bank" will credit "Paris Bank" with £1 million and in their *nostro* account will debit "Paris Bank" with fr. 75 millions.

"London Bank" will receive from the Bank of England through the market £1 million in payment for fr. 75 millions which "London Bank" will have instructed "Paris Bank" to pay to the debit of its account to the Bank of France for account of the Bank of England.

In accordance with the second principle, the E.E.A., through the Bank of England, will surrender the francs to the Bank of France and will receive in exchange the equivalent in gold. This will be "earmarked" for account of the Bank of England or will be shipped to London. The Bank of England will credit the E.E.A. with the gold thus acquired and will debit the E.E.A. with the £1 million paid to "London Bank".

The E.E.A. will obtain the £1 million by discounting, i.e. selling Treasury Bills in the London Money Market to produce this amount. It is possible and quite probable that the buyer of those Treasury Bills is "London Bank", whose deposits have increased by the £1 million remitted by "Paris Bank". The Bank of France in its next weekly statement of its position will show a loss of fr. 75 millions in gold.

The net result of these transactions is a contraction of credit

---

* For convenience only one exchange rate for all transactions is assumed. In practice they would differ to allow for profit.

in France by the loss of fr. 75 millions, and while the E.E.A. has gained gold there is neither an expansion nor contraction in the credit structure in London because the £1 million put into London by French interests has been taken out by the E.E.A. Deposits and discounts of the London banking system have increased, but not the cash basis. The cash ratio has changed, but that is a matter which will be more conveniently dealt with later.

Thus we have the meaning of "offsetting" or neutralising; and also the application of the three basic principles of the E.E.A.: (1) it has prevented a movement of the exchange rate by equating the supply of pounds with the demand, (2) it has obtained gold in exchange for the pounds supplied, and (3) it has prevented an expansion of the credit base.

In the imaginary transaction which we have just described the E.E.A. bought francs and sold sterling, but of course it has often been called upon to operate in the reverse way, i.e. buy sterling and sell francs or some other currency, and no doubt it will be called upon to do so again. It was fortunate for the success of the E.E.A. that in the early months of its life the policy of the Government was such as to inspire confidence at home and abroad. As a consequence a demand for sterling developed. By supplying the sterling the E.E.A. acquired gold (by converting the currencies obtained), which it held as a reserve against the day when it would have to support sterling.

Another assumption which we have made in our hypothetical transaction is that the Bank of England itself bought the francs from "London Bank". In practice this is not always the case. Sometimes it may wish to conceal its operations, in which case it will request other British banks to undertake operations on its behalf. The "Control"* may be in the hands of one bank designated by the Bank of England, or in the hands of several. This is a question of technique which is varied from time to time to fit the circumstances prevailing.

Whether the "Control" is in the hands of the Bank of England at any particular moment or in the hands of one agent or agents,

---

* "Control" is the colloquial term which has come to be used to indicate the E.E.A.

the foreign exchange personnel of the market have no official notification that the operations being conducted by those banks are in fact on behalf of the E.E.A. It is inference only, albeit that it is based on evidence which is regarded as fairly conclusive, especially when, as frequently happens, the Bank of England is the only buyer or the only seller, as the case may be, of a particular currency in which large dealings are taking place at the time.

The transaction outlined above is simple and straightforward. When circumstances change, the technique employed, and even the character of operations of the E.E.A., must change to deal with them. And the circumstances change frequently.

It will be remembered that when Britain suspended the gold standard in 1931 some other countries, notably the Dominions and Scandinavian countries, did the same and linked their currency with sterling. For those countries sterling was the most important currency, and their commercial relationships caused them to elect to keep their currency in line with sterling instead of gold. This group of countries became known as the "sterling bloc", and, as we shall see later, from the point of view of international trade and prices it is a very important group. But there were many other countries which at that time did not follow Britain's example but remained on the gold standard. Of those countries the most important were America, France, Holland and Switzerland, and the countries in this group were referred to as belonging to the "gold bloc". It, too, was a very powerful group. The interplay of forces set going by one group and reacting on the other provided a good deal of controversy, not without some bitterness. In 1934 America made the first breach in the gold bloc by suspending gold payments. Later, Belgium, France, Holland and Switzerland did the same and the gold bloc came to an end. All these events had a direct bearing upon the E.E.A. A table showing the alignment of the principal currencies on 30 June 1938 is given in Appendix K on p. 179. The table is calculated on the rates applicable as at 30 June 1938. But before they attained the comparative stability they possessed at that date there was considerable disturbance.

CHAPTER 4

THE important events mentioned at the end of Chapter 3 changed the character and sometimes the mode of operations of the E.E.A. From the establishment of the Account up to the present time there have been four distinct phases of operations, each succeeding phase being marked by a decisive event in which the cause of the change was inherent. We must make some observations on those phases in their chronological order.

The first phase is bracketed with the establishment of the E.E.A. and the suspension of the gold standard by America in March 1933. During that period there were several important currencies on a gold basis against any or all of which the E.E.A. could operate if it wished. The major control operations took place in the American dollar exchange on account of that currency being the most important from the point of view of the trade of the country. As all other gold currencies were definitely related to the dollar through their gold parities it was possible within limits to control the value of sterling *vis-à-vis* all gold currencies by controlling its relation to the dollar. Subsidiary transactions against gold currencies other than the dollar were undertaken from time to time, but in the main the volume of business done by the E.E.A. was of a size to warrant this phase being described as the dollar phase. The range of the sterling-dollar ratio during this period was \$3·69⅜ and \$3·17, equal to a mean range of about 15 %, which, at first sight, seems to indicate that the E.E.A. was not completely successful in "ironing out" fluctuations. The indictment is partially true and the explanation is this: During the first few months of its existence it was necessary to acquire foreign currencies in order to obtain gold, and not until it had sufficient quantities of gold was it able to work both ways in the Exchange Market. As a seller of sterling it had plenty of resources available. It could not act as a buyer of sterling until it had previously acquired something which the sellers of sterling would accept, and gold alone placed the E.E.A. in that position. In addition, towards the end of 1932, when there was some tension regarding the question of payment of the British War Debt to America, sterling was subject to pressure because of the damage to this country by a refusal to pay, or if an attempt to pay was made, dollars would have to be purchased. The E.E.A. endeavoured to support sterling but, not having had time to acquire sufficient quantities of foreign exchange and gold, it was forced to abandon the attempt, and sterling fell to $3·17 before a recovery set in. These were critical months for the E.E.A., not only from the point of view of its operations but also because of the icy blasts of criticism which descended upon it from many in this country and many more in America. Early in 1933 conditions changed; the E.E.A. was called upon to acquire such large amounts of foreign exchange and gold that a further sum of £200 millions had to be made available to it in May.

The second phase was entered upon when America suspended gold payments and thus deprived holders of dollars of the right to demand gold in exchange for them. The managers of the E.E.A. therefore could not continue to buy dollars which had become a "paper currency". America, in suspending gold payments, was not immediately followed by any of the remaining members of the gold bloc. Next to the dollar in importance was the French franc, and so long as the latter was interchangeable with gold the control's intervention could be safely diverted to that currency in place of the dollar. This was the franc phase, which lasted up to the time of the first devaluation of the French franc in September 1936, the breakdown of the gold bloc and the conclusion of what is now erroneously called the Tripartite Agreement, on which we shall have some observations to make in this and later chapters.

The franc phase was similar to the dollar phase in that during the course of the control's operations in each phase gold was acquired in increasing quantities; or, to express the same thing in another way, sterling came into greater demand as the end of each phase approached. In the first phase the gold came from America; in the second, from France and to a lesser extent from Belgium, Holland and Switzerland. The large influx of capital from these countries caused considerable disturbance to the London Money Market, to meet which the authorities devised a further development of their technique. We shall have occasion to examine this phenomenon at greater length when we come to consider the influence of the E.E.A. on the London Money Market.

Before the breakdown of the gold bloc, America decided in February 1934 to re-link the dollar to gold, not by a fully operated gold standard but by a statutory declaration that the new dollar would be equal to 59·06 cents gold, a ratio which changed the price of one ounce troy of fine gold to $35 as against the former price of $20·67. Internally all gold privately held had to be surrendered to the Government at the original valuation, while externally gold at the new ratio would only be exchanged with those countries operating the gold standard. So that, although the dollar was again attached to gold, the E.E.A. could not operate against that currency because there was no reciprocal arrangement by which gold could be given on demand in this country. Operations therefore were continued in the Continental gold currencies, particularly the French franc.

The devaluation of the French franc and the disintegration of the gold bloc at first seriously threatened the ability of the E.E.A. to control the external value of the pound because, if the principal currencies were no longer interchangeable with gold on demand, the E.E.A. could not operate in those currencies, at least, not with safety. It could to some extent control the value of pounds in terms of gold by going into the open market and buying gold at a price* at which it was desired to establish the pound, but it would have been a very limited control because the amount of gold coming daily to the market at that time was small. The threat, however, was circumvented by another ingenious adaptation of technique, though this time the wisdom

---

* In March 1936 the Belgian currency was re-stabilised on a gold basis, so that a sterling gold price could have been fixed by controlling the belga exchange rate (cf. p. 90).

of the authorities of three great powers was responsible for it. The act referred to was the conclusion of the Tripartite Currency Agreement* on 26 September 1936, which marks the beginning of the third phase.

The Tripartite Currency Agreement, as it originally stood, did not relieve the E.E.A. of the dilemma in which it was placed by the breakdown of the gold bloc referred to above. Nothing in that agreement conformed to the second basic principle under which the E.E.A. operates, viz. currencies could only be acquired if they were convertible to gold. For a few days after the Agreement was made public it was admired for the spirit which actuated the Agreement, as it foreshadowed a willingness on the part of the three countries concerned to forswear competitive currency depreciation for the supposed advantages of such a course. That feature was a very great achievement, but beyond that moral gain there was nothing in the Agreement of a technical nature to give effect to the wishes expressed.

Meanwhile the E.E.A. was dormant, of necessity, as explained. The relief to its dilemma was soon forthcoming and it came in the form of a protocol† to the Tripartite Agreement in which the three powers—America, France and Britain—each agreed to make gold available to the E.E.A. of the other countries, the arrangement being subject to withdrawal by any party to the Agreement on giving 24 hours' notice. It is assumed that the gold, if and when exchanged for currency, would be at a price corresponding to the average exchange rate of the day in question, but there was nothing in the protocol to warrant the assumption. If this were correct, then gold would be subject to transfer by any of the E.E. Accounts at a fluctuating price, a condition which prevailed, so far as the British E.E.A. was concerned, before the collapse of the gold bloc. By this protocol not only was the threat to the E.E.A. removed, but additional power was granted to it by reason of the American dollar becoming available for the E.E.A.'s operations, which hitherto had been impossible for the reasons already explained.

* For the terms of this Agreement see Appendix E.
† See Appendix F.

This phase, then, by operation of the full Agreement, was very similar to the first, as the conditions were restored which enabled the E.E.A. to operate in more than one currency. Later Holland, Switzerland and Belgium signified their willingness to abide by the terms of the original Currency Agreement and the protocol. Thus they formed a new kind of gold bloc held together on a 24-hour basis, affording mutual support by denying themselves vicarious assistance in the shape of competitive currency depreciation and granting mutual facilities in gold, without which the Agreement would have no practical value.

In this phase we find the E.E.A. operating "with elbow room" in a considerably enlarged sphere and with a denser screen to its operations because it frequently happened that, although it was known in the Exchange Market that the Bank of England was intervening, it was not known outside official quarters whether those operations were undertaken on behalf of the British E.E.A. or that of one of the adherents to the Currency Agreement. From all points of view—volume of transactions, gold acquired, temporary disturbance to domestic Money Market, etc.—this phase was of the greatest importance. In the main the attention of the managers of the Account was occupied with the vicissitudes of the French franc, which during the period was subject to two devaluations and finally severed from gold on a statutory basis and left to find its own level. The phase ended with the efflux of capital to France in May 1938, producing the obverse of the conditions which prevailed during the previous phase when French capital sought safety in London.

The fourth phase began with the "Daladier franc"—so called after the Prime Minister of France who was responsible for the statement that the franc would not be allowed to fall below 179 to the pound. The initiative in exchange controls passed to the French, who were placed in that position by the sudden return of French capital amounting to the equivalent of £120 millions. The British E.E.A. was more active on its own account in the Money Market than in the Exchange Market, in which it was merely acting as the agent for the French control. Its ingenuity was called upon during the early part of this phase in devising expedients to minimise the disturbance to the credit structure by the sudden withdrawal from London of an amount estimated at £80 millions in the space of a few days, immediately following the establishment of the Daladier franc. The withdrawal of such a large sum at such short notice under a gold standard system or a managed currency system without an E.E.A. would have produced a crisis of some magnitude. In this instance, under the conditions and technique built up during the six years of the E.E.A., the withdrawal has become notable by reason of the ease and smoothness of the offsetting operations and the complete absence of apprehension in the minds of those immediately concerned and by the general public. The latter was quite unaware of what was taking place, although its interests would have been vitally compromised had the arrangements broken down.

With the completion of the withdrawal and the consequent offsetting operations (which were spread over four or five weeks) and the initiative for intervention in the Exchange Market in the hands of the French authorities, the British E.E.A. has been called upon to act in a very minor way, usually in the dollar. Its activities have been more decisive in another market—the Gold Market—in which it has achieved a monopolistic position by its ability to supply the quantities required or to absorb the amounts on offer, and by virtue of that position it dominates the price. Since the dollar has a fixed relation to gold ($35 an ounce), and as the sterling price of gold can be regulated at will by the E.E.A., the dollar-sterling ratio is thereby indirectly controlled. By determining the size of the premium* in the sterling gold price over the dollar shipping parity, it decides two things: (1) whether gold in the open market shall be bought by arbitrageurs who anticipate making a profit by shipment to America, and (2) whether sterling shall be allowed to rise or fall in terms of dollars. Within the compass of the aggregate of the premium and discount on the shipping parity, which amounts to about 1s. 11d. per ounce, and a fairly stable dollar exchange

---

* For an explanation of the premium or discount in the sterling price of gold see p. 88.

rate, the E.E.A. can maintain the value of sterling in terms of gold, and the basis seems to be (although there is no legal mandate for it) about £7 per ounce. We must defer to a later chapter observations that should be made on the advantages or dangers that there may be in the policy of the E.E.A. controlling the value of sterling in terms of gold as distinct from controlling its value in terms of foreign currencies, particularly the dollar, which primarily was its *raison d'être*.

Here we are concerned with that part of the E.E.A. policy providing the feature of the period which we are describing as the fourth phase. Some writers went so far as to describe this phase as the development of a new type of gold standard with the limit of about £7. 0s. 6d. for the upper and about £6. 19s. 6d. for the lower gold price. It is well to remember, however, that the technique employed and the principles adopted by the E.E.A. have undergone changes, some of which we have considered, and it is possible that conditions in the future may call for further changes designed to meet the conditions then obtaining.*

* Further changes were in fact necessary as a result of the September crisis (see Chapter 13, p. 120).

RÉSUMÉ OF PART I

We have described the events and some of the causes which led up to the suspension of the gold standard in Britain in September 1931, and we have explained the need for some regulating agency and how the E.E.A. was designed for that purpose. Having stated the main principles under which the E.E.A. operates we have enquired into the developing nature of the technique employed and found that there are four distinct phases in its life since its inception. We have mentioned the chief features of each phase. They can be described as:

1. The dollar phase.
2. The franc phase.
3. The Tripartite Agreement phase.
4. The gold phase.

It is understood that the terms used in describing the phases are not exclusive in the sense that no other operations were undertaken during the period, but that they describe the broad characteristics of the phase.

In Part II we must examine in detail the method by which the E.E.A. provides itself with the sterling resources and how it prevents any disturbance to the credit structure of the country by an influx or efflux of foreign fugitive capital, particularly the immigration of large amounts of French capital during the period April to July 1936 and the sudden emigration of that money in May 1938.

In the following four chapters our interest will be directed to the London Money Market, which is the scene of those influences providing the objective of Part II.

PART II

CHAPTER 5

A PROPER understanding of the mechanism of the E.E.A., especially in regard to its offsetting operations—a description of which is our next objective—is quite impossible without some knowledge of the Bank of England's weekly statement, the meaning of the changes in the figures therein, and the relation and bearing of those changes on the Money Market.

For the benefit of those who are not familiar with the statement, this chapter attempts to explain as briefly as possible the essential points. Readers who possess this knowledge are invited to ignore this chapter and turn to Chapter 6, p. 39, where the narrative of the E.E.A. is resumed.

The Bank of England Weekly Statement

The Bank Charter Act 1844 required the Bank of England to issue each week a statement setting forth the current position of assets and liabilities of the Issue and Banking Departments respectively. The Currency and Bank Notes Act 1928 modified the form in which the statement is issued, although the principal provisions of the earlier Act were maintained. A statement in the new form is here reproduced and a brief explanation given of the items mentioned therein. Numbers in brackets have been inserted to facilitate reference in the text which follows.

BANK OF ENGLAND   27 *April* 1938

ISSUE DEPARTMENT

Liabilities	£	*Assets*	£
tes issued:		(3) Government debt	11,015,100
(1) In circulation	489,261,893	(4) Other Government securities	188,602,945
(2) In Banking Department	37,145,267	(5) Other securities	373,168
		(6) Silver coin	8,787
		(7) Amount of Fiduciary Issue	200,000,000
		(8) Gold-coin and bullion ...	326,407,160
Total £526,407,160		Total £526,407,160	

BANKING DEPARTMENT

	Liabilities		£		*Assets*		£
(9)	Proprietors' capital	...	14,553,000	(14)	Government securities	...	113,996,16
(10)	Rest	...	3,157,552		Other securities:		
(11)	Public deposits*	...	10,889,533	(15)	Discounts and advances	...	7,063,68
	Other deposits:			(16)	Securities	...	19,379,55
(12)	Bankers ...	...	113,288,096	(17)	Notes	...	37,145,26
(13)	Other accounts	...	36,512,509	(18)	Gold and silver coin	...	816,01
		Total	£178,400,690			Total	£178,400,69

* Including Exchequer, Savings Banks, Commissioners of National Debt, Dividend Accounts an Exchange Equalisation Account.

Lord Overstone, the chief promoter of the Act of 1844 (sometimes referred to as Peel's Act), stated that the Bank "acts in two capacities—(1) as a manager of the circulation, and (2) as a body performing the ordinary functions of a banking concern". Hence the reason for issuing the statement in two parts—Issue Department and Banking Department.

Issue Department

On the liabilities side of the statement under the heading "Issue Department" there is mentioned the amount of notes issued (1) in circulation, and (2) in the Banking Department. The last term corresponds to the amount given on the assets side under the heading of "Banking Department" and described as "Notes" (17). The connection between these items in the two departments will be considered later.

On the assets side, "Government Debt" (3) is the amount which is owing by the Government to the Bank of England. This item has become frozen. Under the Bank Charter Act, if this debt is ever repaid by the Government, the Bank of England would lose its Charter.

"Other Government Securities" (4) consist of British Government securities, and with "Other Securities" (5) constitute the earning assets of the department. Item (6) is self-explanatory. The Currency and Bank Notes Act 1928 stipulates that the amount of silver coin held by the Bank in this department must not exceed £5,500,000. The same Act also ensures that the profits of this department accrue to the Treasury. The Issue Department of the Bank of England is therefore indistinguishable from a Government Department.

Items (3) to (6) make a total of £200,000,000 which constitutes the "Fiduciary Issue", i.e. that part of the total note issue uncovered by gold. The Currency and Bank Notes Act* stipulates that the Fiduciary Issue must not exceed £260,000,000 without definite authority from the Treasury, and any minute from the Treasury authorising an increase must be laid before Parliament. A reduction of £60 millions in the Fiduciary Issue was made in December 1936 when the E.E.A. sold gold for that amount to the Issue Department.† The difference between the total Fiduciary Issue on the assets side and the total liabilities is made up by item (8) "Gold coin and bullion". The gold which makes up the increase in the Bank's holdings since June 1932 has been obtained from the E.E.A.‡

Banking Department

The capital (9) of the Bank in 1833 was £14,553,000 and has since remained unchanged. This meagre capital and the limited other resources of the Bank were reasons for establishing another agent with larger capital resources to cope with the problems which arose out of the gold standard suspension in 1931; hence the formation of the E.E.A.

Item (10), "Rest" or surplus, is an accumulation of undivided profits and does not ever fall below £3 millions. Profits of the Banking Department accrue to shareholders, subject to setting aside such sums therefrom as are required in the public interest and for public uses. The amount for distribution to shareholders is paid out of this account.

"Public Deposits" (11) consists of balances standing to the credit of various Government Departments, including the E.E.A., and such balances fluctuate considerably with the flow of national revenue and expenditure and the operations of the E.E.A. "Public Deposits" (11) and "Bankers' Deposits" (12) are important and are frequently referred to in the remaining chapters.

* See Addenda, p. 143.   † Cf. p. 86.   ‡ Cf. p. 83.

"Bankers' Deposits" (12) are the balances kept at the Bank of England by the clearing banks,* and form part of their cash reserves, since a credit balance at the Bank of England entitles the creditor to draw cash (notes) if and when required. There is no compulsion on the clearing banks to keep balances with the Bank of England, but if they wish to have the advantages which obtain from membership of the Bankers' Clearing House they must maintain such balances. The item "Bankers' Deposits" is a very clear indication of the state of the Money Market, as will be explained later.

Item (13), "Other Accounts", is the total of funds standing to the credit of customers, other than H.M. Government, on current or deposit account; it includes Empire and foreign Central Banks, the Indian and Colonial financial authorities and such commercial accounts as still survive in the Bank of England from the days when it was in active competition with other banks.

On the assets side, "Government Securities" (14) represents the Bank's investment in Treasury Bills, Exchequer Bonds and other British Government securities, while "Discounts and Advances" (15) comprises bills discounted and advances made to the Bank's regular clients. "Securities" (16) includes purchases of first-class commercial bills. Items (17) and (18) need no explanation, but are very important.

The weekly statement is issued on Thursdays, showing the position as at close on Wednesday. It arouses much interest at home and abroad and is carefully examined by all whose duties require them to keep a close touch on the financial pulse. The statement is an instantaneous "photograph" of the position at a stated time of the week, and is out-of-date almost as soon as it has been compiled, a feature common to most balance-sheets.

The statement shows four features: (a) the position of the Bank of England as banker to the Government, (b) the state of

* Walter Leaf in *Banking*, Chapter III: "The Bank of England is the centre not only of the national finance, as the sole bank of issue and controlling the currency in partnership with the Treasury, but is also the centre of the general deposit banking system of the country, by its position as the banker of the banks in which capacity it holds the ultimate reserve of the whole system of joint-stock banking."

the national currency, (c) the Bank of England as a bankers' bank, and (d) the Bank of England as banker to private customers. Such a mixture of functions is unique in Central Banking practice.

When the statement is published it is examined by those interested for any changes that may have been made since the previous week, especially in the Reserve of the Bank of England, i.e. the liquid fund available that can be drawn upon at a moment's notice. When a gold standard is operated the Reserve item is very carefully watched because the rise or fall of the Reserve is often a forerunner of a fall or rise in Bank Rate. Under the present managed currency regime the Reserve does not occupy the same place of importance because the Bank of England's gold stock is protected in other ways, for instance, by operations of the E.E.A. Items (17) and (18) form the Reserve; the proportion the Reserve bears to total deposits is the important factor, and that can be ascertained by a simple calculation:

$$\frac{\text{Reserve} \times 100}{\text{Deposits}} = \text{``Proportion''}$$

(17)	37,145,267	
(18)	816,018	
Reserve	£ 37,961,285 × 100	
		= 23·6 %
(11)	10,889,533	
(12)	113,288,096	
(13)	36,512,509	
Deposits	£160,690,138	

As the figure for Bankers' Deposits represents the cash reserves of the commercial deposit banks maintaining accounts with the Bank of England which are drawn upon in times of stringency, the Bank is very vulnerable.* In gold standard days

---

* The Bank Charter Act of 1844 gave to the Bank of England not only its authority but its strength and safeguards for an emergency as opposed to its many weaknesses before the existence of the Act, and placed this country as the first to operate the gold standard, in the modern sense of the term (see Glossary). It is a curious fact that when the emergencies have come the only relief obtainable has been through the suspension or part suspension of the Act itself. Full convertibility of notes for gold as established in the Act has been suspended no less than five times: in 1847, 1857, 1866, 1914 and 1931. Without these suspensions the reserves of the Bank of England would have vanished overnight.

the Bank maintained a very high ratio of cash to deposits, much higher than is customary by the commercial banks, which is about 10%. As the Bank is now reinforced by the E.E.A. with large resources, the reserve is at times allowed to run down to quite a low figure without causing undue uneasiness. During the September 1938 crisis and aftermath the "proportion" as shown in the weekly statement* was 13·8%, but it is probable that the "proportion" was very much lower during the few days prior to the issue of the statement. The "proportion" must not be confused with the percentage called the "Reserve ratio" which is the ratio of gold holdings in both departments to the total of deposits and notes in circulation. Thus in the statement on pp. 29 and 30 there appears:

Assets

		£
In the Issue Department		
(8) Gold coin and bullion		326,407,160
In the Banking Department		
(18) Gold and silver coin		816,018
		£327,223,178

Liabilities

		£
In the Issue Department		
(1) Notes in circulation		489,261,893
In the Banking Department		
(11) Public Deposits		10,889,533
(12) Bankers' Deposits		113,288,096
(13) Other accounts		36,512,509
		£649,952,031

$$\frac{£327,223,178 \times 100}{£649,952,031} = 50\cdot34\% \text{ "Reserve ratio"}.$$

The "proportion" is the measure of the Bank of England's liquidity and under a gold standard regime is the key to movements in Bank Rate. Under the present regime there is not the same importance attached to the size of the "proportion" and the movements of Bank Rate are not now dependent on the amount of the Reserve.

* 5 October 1938.

Bank Rate, which is ordinarily made known at noon on Thursday of each week, is the minimum rate at which the Bank of England will discount approved bills. In emergencies the Court of Directors of the Bank have changed Bank Rate on other days of the week. Since 30 June 1932, Bank Rate has remained at 2%. Under a gold standard regime Bank Rate plays a very important part in regulating the supply of credit and the import or export of capital.

The following are the main enactments which govern the operations of the Bank of England at the present time:

The Bank Charter Act 1844 obliges the Bank of England to buy gold at 77s. 9d. per standard troy ounce.* This price was confirmed by the Currency and Bank Notes Act 1928.† Notwithstanding the suspension of the gold standard in 1931, this obligation to buy gold at the stipulated price, if it is offered, is still in force.* The Gold Standard Act 1925‡ established the Bank of England's selling price of 77s. 10½d. per standard troy ounce, and provided for the convertibility of notes to bar gold, of about 400 fine ounces, on demand. The Gold Standard Act 1925 was suspended on 21 September 1931 by the Gold Standard (Amendment) Act 1931,§ after which the obligation to sell gold at the stated price ceased to be effective. There is one qualification to the prohibition placed on the Bank of England by the 1931 Act. The Finance Act 1932 contains clauses authorising the establishment of the E.E.A. Clause 25‖ of that Act, Sections 2(a) and 3, allows for sales and purchases of gold by the Bank of England to and from the E.E.A. and stipulates that such transactions must be carried out on the basis of the fixed price of 77s. 10½d. per standard troy ounce.*

Here it will be an advantage if we consider what happens when an import of gold takes place when a gold standard is operated.

By reason of the fact that a credit balance with the Bank of England may be used in the withdrawal of notes, the balances maintained at the Bank of England by the clearing banks are regarded by them as the equivalent of cash and are shown as

* See Addenda, p. 143.   † See Appendix B.   ‡ See Appendix A.
§ See Appendix C.   ‖ See Appendix D.

such in their balance-sheets. The clearing bank balances are included in the Bank of England's weekly statement under the heading of "Bankers' Deposits" (12), and they form part of the liabilities of the Bank of England against which it holds a reserve in the most liquid form, i.e. in notes, and the proportion such reserve bears to bankers' and other deposits varies from day to day. Under a gold standard, as operated between 1925 and 1931, any person with the required quantity of notes could present them to the Issue Department and obtain a bar or bars of gold on demand. The clearing banks, if they wished, could draw cheques on the Bank of England for the quantity of bar gold they wanted to buy for themselves or for their clients. Such a transaction would change the balances in both Departments of the Bank of England. Let us examine just how this happens, bearing in mind that we are discussing for a moment the operations as they were carried out when the gold standard was in operation.

A clearing bank, for example, presents to the Banking Department a cheque drawn on its balance with the Bank of England and obtains notes. As a consequence the item "Bankers' Deposits" (12) will fall, and on the other side of the account the item "Notes" (17) will fall by an equal amount. The clearing bank then presents the notes to the Issue Department and obtains gold bars. The Issue Department thereupon cancels the notes received, and the amount for notes in circulation is correspondingly reduced and a reduction of a like amount is recorded in the item "Gold coin and bullion".

On the other hand, if gold is sold to the Bank of England, Bankers' Deposits and notes in the Banking Department will rise, and "Gold coin and bullion" and "Notes in circulation" in the Issue Department will also rise.

These transactions can be shown diagrammatically, thus:

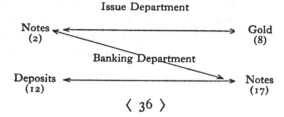

When gold is bought from the Bank of England the "proportion" will fall; when gold is sold to the Bank a rise is recorded in "proportion", unless sold against a reduction in the Fiduciary Issue.

It will be understood from the foregoing that owners of sterling balances in a gold standard regime had the means of withdrawing gold from the Bank of England and, if desired, exporting it. Consequently if conditions here were such that foreigners holding sterling balances became nervous or if they thought they could employ their funds to better advantage elsewhere, the Bank of England would have had many claims upon its gold stock. If the Bank considered it advisable to take steps to protect its gold stock, the first measure of defence is by what is known as "open-market operations". In the Banking Department on the assets side there is shown an item "Government Securities" (14). This is the item which reflects open-market operations. The Bank of England will sell some of those securities —Treasury Bills to the Money Market or to the Public Departments, and longer dated securities on the Stock Exchange. By such action the Bank of England will ultimately receive payment through the clearing banks, and therefore Bankers' Deposits will decline on one side of its accounts and Government securities on the other. The Bank, as a consequence of such operations, withdraws funds from the market and money rates will tend to harden. If money can be more profitably employed in London there will be less demand for gold for export.

When the Bank wishes to expand the cash fund by open-market operations, Government securities are bought and Bankers' Deposits are thereby increased. These open-market operations do not have any direct effect on the amount of the Reserve of the Bank, so that as Bankers' Deposits rise or fall with purchases or sales of securities by the Bank of England, the "proportion" will fall or rise to correspond.

It is obvious that defence of the Bank's gold stocks by open-market operations is limited to a proportion of the resources at its disposal. If losses of gold continued the Bank of England would then adopt its second line of defence—a rise in Bank

Rate. As all other interest rates are governed by Bank Rate, a rise in the latter sets in motion a whole series of adjustments in the financial and economic machinery. When these adjustments have been completed and capital from abroad begins to flow in, Bank Rate will be lowered, to which change all other interest rates will conform.

The foregoing explains very briefly what happens under a gold standard regime. The Bank of England does not now defend its gold stock by open-market operations or by a rise in Bank Rate. The E.E.A. accumulates gold in a separate account and sells it whenever required at a price which the E.E.A. is in a position to influence, except when gold is sold to the Bank of England.

The open-market operations of the Bank of England are still carried out and are just as important as they were in gold standard days. For instance, the Bank of England nearly always offsets a withdrawal of notes by a purchase of Government securities and a return of notes by a sale. In this way the supply of cash is constantly kept under control. Open-market operations form a large part of the offsetting functions of the E.E.A., and as it has very large resources the control of the authorities over the credit base of the country is very nearly absolute.

The open-market operations of the E.E.A. are explained more fully in later chapters.

CHAPTER 6

IN addition to the constituents of the sphere of operations of the E.E.A. which we have already considered, i.e. the Bank of England and the commercial banks, there is also the Money Market* consisting of banks, discount houses and bill brokers, the Gold Market and the Stock Exchange. The last two may be disposed of quickly. The Gold Market is an entirely free market in which foreigners and foreign Central Banks may buy and sell gold. In addition, gold may be bought by persons in this country but no individual may hold more than the equivalent of £10,000. Gold is also bought for industry and the arts. In this free market the E.E.A. operates as a buyer or as a seller. On account of the magnitude of its gold operations the E.E.A. occupies a dominant position. In the Stock Exchange the Bank of England buys or sells securities on its own account through the usual channels, but the reason for such buying or selling may lie in the offsetting operations carried out on behalf of the E.E.A., a point which will be elaborated later on.

The London Money Market, or that part of it with which we are particularly concerned—the short-loan market—is the first line of defence of the commercial banks, of whose funds a certain proportion must be maintained in a highly liquid form, in loans at call and in loans at short notice. As collateral for those

* "The London Money Market is capable of several definitions. In its widest sense it comprises the whole machinery for the provision of credit and finance to the British Isles and the Empire, and indeed to the outside world. In this sense it embraces the Bank of England as its hub; the British clearing and other joint-stock banks and the Dominion and foreign banks; the accepting houses and merchant bankers who combine the acceptance of bills of exchange with the floating of long-term loans; the discount houses and bill-brokers; and to a certain extent the Stock Exchange, the insurance companies and all those engaged in industry, commerce and shipping. In short it comprises every potential lender and borrower. In the narrower sense, however, the money market is regarded primarily as the market dealing in bills of exchange, and it is then often called the discount market." ("The Evolution of the Money Market", by Norman Crump, *Journal of the Institute of Bankers*, June 1938.)

loans bills are pledged—bank bills of exchange and Treasury Bills. In times of strain the banks call in money from the short-loan market; the discount houses and bill brokers who are called upon to repay to the banks must go to the Bank of England for funds if they are unable to provide them themselves. The Bank of England is therefore the "lender of last resort" which will only discount bills at Bank Rate or lend against them for a minimum of eight days at $\frac{1}{2}\%$ above.

It is by manipulation of the short-loan fund that the Bank of England maintains its control over the Money Market, and by withdrawing or creating credit it is the arbiter of its price.

Nowadays bank bills form only a small part of the collateral of the short-loan market, Treasury Bills being the principal stock-in-trade. The Treasury Bill is an ingenious device invented to meet the needs of the Government by affording a cheap means of borrowing for short-term periods. It also meets the needs of all those constituents of the Money Market who have money to lend for short periods to a borrower of unimpeachable integrity. At the same time it provides them with a security which is immediately acceptable as collateral should they wish to turn borrowers. Recent history has confirmed the standing of the Treasury Bill as the highest in the world. It enables the Government to borrow up to £1000 millions at a cost to it of only about £5,000,000 per annum.

There are two issues of Treasury Bills—"tender" and "tap". "Tender" bills are tendered for each week by the market and are allotted up to the amount previously announced and to the tenderers who offer the best price. The Government borrows money at the best possible rate by putting lenders in competition with one another. Tender bills are issued for a term of 90 or 91 days.

"Tap" bills are available on tap for the several departments of Government which are in funds and wish to lend them, and if required are issued for a period less than 90 or 91 days. Such departments as the Post Office, the National Health Insurance, the National Debt Commissioners, Exchange Equalisation

Account, the Bank of England, etc., all have funds for temporary periods, and if they were left idle on deposit with the Bank of England the credit structure of the country would be contracted. The Government is therefore a large lender as well as a large borrower, a position which gives it a predominant influence in the finances of the country. In matters of the supply of credit and its price the Government has the last word, and since 1931 it has exercised that power in no uncertain fashion, maintaining a plentiful supply on the cheapest terms for a length of time unparalleled.

At the beginning of its operations the E.E.A. was supplied with £150 millions worth of "tap" Treasury Bills, and further amounts of £200 millions in May 1933 and July 1937 respectively. The amount of the floating debt in the form of Treasury Bills was increased by these amounts. The E.E.A. retains possession of the bills issued to it until it wishes to operate in the exchange market. The total amount of Treasury Bills held by the E.E.A. is therefore its potential borrowing power, which it will convert to actual borrowing only to the extent that foreigners release gold in exchange for sterling above the normal commercial requirements. By this mechanism the Government borrows the money which foreigners send here for refuge and place on deposit, and by such borrowing prevents any expansion of the credit base which otherwise would take place.

Let us now observe the E.E.A. in action and let us assume the same set of circumstances and the same operations as described on p. 16 when we set out to show primarily the several transactions involving the Foreign Exchange Market whenever the E.E.A. undertakes operations in accordance with its mandate. We are now concerned with the E.E.A. from the point of view of the effects of its operations on the Money Market and the mechanism employed.

"Monsieur Blank" has remitted his capital to London, and in exchange for his francs he has now got £1 million on deposit; whether it is in his own name with a bank in London, or held in London in the name of his French banker on his behalf, is immaterial. A London banking agent, say the "London Bank", has had its deposits increased by the amount, and if that agent maintains the usual ratio of 10% cash to deposits its potential lending capacity has increased by £900,000. "London Bank" was placed in receipt of that £1 million by the sale of the francs to the Bank of England, which we must presume was working on behalf of the E.E.A. The E.E.A. must find in sterling the whole amount it has paid away for the francs; it will therefore sell £1 million of its assets, i.e. Treasury Bills, to those constituents of the Money Market which have money available. This may be described as the primary offsetting operation. Now we have seen that "London Bank" has money to lend, at least up to £900,000, and it finds it convenient to lend that money to the Government, receiving in exchange a gilt-edged instrument which is "near cash" because of its high liquidity. So now the position with "London Bank" is: its deposits have gone up by £1,000,000, and on the other side of the balance-sheet discounts have increased by £900,000, so that its cash ratio is unaltered. The E.E.A. must obtain the balance of £100,000 from some other constituent of the market. If "London Bank" does not wish to purchase any Treasury Bills, the whole amount must be obtained elsewhere. The net effect of borrowing the total amount from the market as a whole is: the cash ratios of the banking system have declined by reason of the fact that deposits and discounts have increased while cash is unchanged. "London Bank" if it wished could have loaned the available money at call or at short notice instead of buying Treasury Bills, in which event the balance-sheet item affected would be that for "Loans at call and short notice". Again, the net effect on the market as a whole is a reduction in the cash ratio. What effect, if any, has this operation had on the balance-sheet of the Bank of England?

If "London Bank" keeps an account with the Bank of England it will have been credited with the £1 million in payment for the francs bought by the E.E.A. The item "Bankers' Deposits" will therefore increase. "London Bank" and others will have been debited with the amounts of their purchases of Treasury Bills, and "Bankers' Deposits" will thus have been restored to its original position.

Let us illustrate these transactions:

Stage I

The relevant entries before the above operation were:

BANK OF ENGLAND (Banking Department)

Public Deposits	£7 millions	Notes and coin	£58 millions
Bankers' Deposits	£104 ,,		
Other deposits	£38 ,,	The "proportion" is 39·3 %	

"LONDON BANK"

Deposits	£5 millions	Cash	£500,000
		Bills discounted ⎫	
		or ⎬	£750,000
		Loans at call and ⎭	
		short notice	
		Cash ratio is 10 %	

Stage II

The E.E.A.* pays £1 million for the francs bought and "London Bank" creates a deposit for "Monsieur Blank":

BANK OF ENGLAND

Public Deposits	£6 millions	Notes and coin	£58 millions
Bankers' Deposits	£105 ,,		
Other deposits	£38 ,,	The "proportion" is 39·3 %	

"LONDON BANK"

Deposits	£6 millions	Cash	£1,500,000
		Bills discounted ⎫	
		or ⎬	£750,000
		Loans at call ⎭	
		Cash ratio is 25 %	

Stage III

The E.E.A. sells Treasury Bills, "London Bank" buys them, to the extent of £1 million. (To show the effect on the market as a whole we are assuming that "London Bank" buys the whole amount.)

BANK OF ENGLAND

Public Deposits	£7 millions	Notes and coin	£58 millions
Bankers' Deposits	£104 ,,		
Other deposits	£38 ,,	The "proportion" is 39·3 %	

* The banking account of the E.E.A. is maintained in "Public Deposits" of the Bank of England.

⟨ 43 ⟩

"LONDON BANK

Deposits	£6 millions	Cash	£500,000
		Bills discounted ⎫	
		or ⎬	£1,750,000
		Loans at call ⎭	
		Cash ratio is **8·33** %	

These skeleton balance-sheets show that finally the Bank of England's position is unchanged while that of "London Bank" has had its deposits and bills discounted increased. If "London Bank" loaned the money to the short-loan market against Treasury Bills the item "Loans at call" would have been increased instead of "Bills discounted". The cash item, on balance, has undergone no change in amount, and in consequence the ratio of cash to deposit liabilities has fallen to 8·33 %, and it will remain at that reduced level until the Treasury Bills which it has bought mature or the deposit is repaid or its cash increased by some other means.

In regard to the Bank of England it will be noticed that the "proportion" is unchanged throughout because the only items altered are Public Deposits and Bankers' Deposits. When the E.E.A. paid out the £1 million, the Bank of England debited the E.E.A. in its books and thus reduced the balance of Public Deposits. When the E.E.A. received funds for Treasury Bills sold in the market, the E.E.A. was credited, and therefore Public Deposits increased.

At Stage II the "proportion" of cash to Bankers' Deposits only has fallen, but as positive withdrawal of deposits may take place in Public as well as Bankers' Deposits it is not right to ignore Public Deposits when assessing the reserve. (At this stage the parallel with the effect produced by an import of gold under a gold standard is exact. The rise in Bankers' Deposits has potentially enlarged the credit base by ten times the amount of the increase. This, however, is not the end of the cycle of operations under the present monetary regime.)

But, suppose that the E.E.A. had sold its Treasury Bills to the Bank of England instead of to the market, which is a likely supposition because, being the London banker of other Central Banks, it must have funds to invest from time to time in the same way as other bankers. In this case, as in the former, Public Deposits would show a rise but the compensating item would be on the other side of the balance-sheet in the item (14) "Government Securities", and therefore the "proportion" would fall. As the managers of the E.E.A. would not wish to immobilise funds by leaving them on deposit with the Bank of England, sooner or later that £1 million would be put back into the market by reducing the tender issue of Treasury Bills and so produce a rise in Bankers' Deposits at the expense of Public Deposits. The "proportion", however, would remain the same until the Bank of England sold the Treasury Bills acquired. A purchase by the Bank of England of Treasury Bills or any other security eventually expands the cash basis of the money market. A sale of securities by the Bank sooner or later contracts the cash supply.

Returning to the position of "London Bank" we have observed that, by its participations in the exchange and the money market counterpart, its ratio of cash to deposit liabilities has fallen. That is to say that the influx of foreign capital has produced a deflationary effect on the credit structure in this country. That is precisely the opposite effect to that produced by an influx of capital (gold) under a fully operated gold standard. Let us be quite sure on the point by reviewing the circumstances and effects of incoming gold under the system in operation between 1925 and 1931. Ignoring inessential items the chain of effects produced by a gold import was as follows:

The gold was consigned to a London bank for the credit of somebody's account somewhere. On receipt, the London bank took the gold to the Issue Department of the Bank of England and received in exchange the equivalent in notes. The notes were taken to the Banking Department, where they were paid in to the credit of the account of the London bank. The effect so far was a rise in the figures of gold held on the assets side of the Issue Department and, on the liabilities, a rise in notes issued. In the Banking Department, assets were increased by the notes received from the London bank, and liabilities by the increase in deposits. The "proportion" of the reserve to deposits has widened.

In the meantime the London bank's cash figures increased by the amount deposited with the Bank of England, and to the same extent its liabilities by the credit opened for the gold received. The ratio of cash to liabilities for this bank were increased also. By these operations the credit basis of the system here was increased by a much greater extent than the actual value of the gold imported.*

It is clear therefore that an influx of capital from abroad under a gold standard system leads to an expansion, and that an influx under a managed currency system such as we have had in operation since 1931 leads to a contraction in credit.

But we have stated and, it is hoped, demonstrated that the third principle under which the E.E.A. operates is to take precise action to prevent any such contraction or expansion taking place following the import or export of capital.

Two things must be said in explanation. Firstly, we are aware that "London Bank's" *ratio* of cash to liabilities has been reduced but not the *amount* of its cash. The ratio is changed by reason of the increase in deposits, which are compensated on the other side of the balance-sheet by an increase in bills discounted or loans at call and short notice. So that, widening the scope to include the whole market, if the *amount* of cash held by the banks be unchanged by the influx of capital, the potential deflationary forces which are made apparent by the reduced ratio do not become *actual* unless the demand for credit is being denied by reason of the existence of the reduced ratio. The amount of cash for internal credit purposes is the same after an influx of foreign capital offset by the E.E.A. as before it. If the potential credit is not used to the fullest extent warranted by the cash available, it cannot be said that there is deflation when there is no change in the amount of cash but only a decline in the percentage that cash bears to the sight liabilities. As Walter Leaf has well said "...the amount of their reserves is not the cause, but the effect, of their ability to give credit".†

Secondly, when it does become established that the piling up of deposits in the banking system without any change in the

* See remarks on Stage II, p. 44.   † *Op. cit.* Chapter V, p. 134.

total amount of cash has become restrictive, then further and fuller measures* must be and are undertaken to relieve the position. The way to provide that relief is to inject more cash into the money system and that can be done best by the Bank of England, whose funds, though small compared with those of the clearing banks, are nevertheless marginal, which gives them a leverage that is decisive. The injection of cash may be accomplished in several ways. The classical method and the speediest is the purchase of Government securities by the Banking Department. The increase in securities is balanced by an increase in Bankers' Deposits. Although this method is very effective it is limited to the resources available in the Banking Department. If the notes in that Department are down to a low level or if the conditions in the Money Market which have produced the stringency are likely to exist for more than a temporary period,† then one of the two following methods may be adopted. Firstly, the Bank of England can request the Treasury to authorise an increase in the Fiduciary Issue, and as the Treasury has power under the Currency and Bank Notes Act of 1928‡ to grant such requests if it approves, it is probable that it would do so. With the authority obtained the Bank of England may issue new notes up to the amount authorised by the Treasury without any backing of additional gold. Thus, the reserve of the Bank of England will be increased and, of course, its "proportion". The second method is for the E.E.A. to sell some of its gold to the Bank of England which would then be in a position to issue notes up to the value of the gold newly acquired. Either method produces more cash in the Bank of England; but the additional credit is wanted in the commercial banking system. That again can be ensured by appropriate action of the Bank of England and of the E.E.A. The latter, instead of borrowing sterling by issues of Treasury Bills to pay for subsequent purchases of gold and/or foreign exchange, may pay for those purchases out of the sterling it has received by the sale of gold to the Bank of England; or the

* Described in Chapters 7 and 8.   † Cf. p. 58.
‡ See Appendix B.

E.E.A. may purchase bills or securities direct from the market. A debit to Public Deposits and a credit to Bankers' Deposits, bringing about a rise in the volume of cash of the commercial banks, would complete the series of operations designed to restore the cash ratios of the banking system. Any of these methods, which may be described as secondary offsetting operations, would be undertaken only if the contraction in credit had not been corrected normally by a reverse movement of capital or if the banks, in order to restore their ratios, embarked upon a course of active deflation by allowing their bill portfolios to be reduced, or called in advances.

There emerge from the foregoing certain principles:

1. Under the present monetary regime the immediate effects of gold acquisitions are apparently deflationary; they reduce cash ratios by increasing deposits, leaving the *amount* of cash unchanged. The immediate effects of gold exports are apparently inflationary; they increase cash ratios by decreasing deposits, leaving the *amount* of cash unchanged. These phenomena are precisely the opposite of those produced by a fully operated gold standard system.

2. When the E.E.A. intervenes it carries out a double operation. It buys or sells foreign exchange in the Foreign Exchange Market and it borrows or repays cash in the Money Market corresponding to the exchange operation. Ultimately further operations may be undertaken to offset an accumulated potential credit stringency, and that can be done either by a manipulation of the Fiduciary Issue or by the E.E.A. selling or buying gold direct to and from the Bank of England. The second alternative is more probable.

3. The Bank of England's influence in the short-loan fund, and through it the whole credit structure, is very nearly absolute, governed only by the size of its gold holdings and securities. By comparison with the whole banking system the funds available to the Bank of England are small, but being marginal they are decisive in effect. This was true under gold standard regime. Under the present regime of a managed currency the degree of control over the quantity and price of credit is very

much greater. The increased power is derived from its position as agent for the E.E.A. which is another way of stating that the control of credit is now one of the functions of Government.

4. The reactions of gold imports or exports under a gold standard system were largely automatic. Offsetting by open-market operations by the Bank of England was very limited, especially in times of emergency when there would be need for offsetting operations of some magnitude. Under the present system of managed currency, with the E.E.A. as an integral part of that system, the reactions of gold imports and exports are a matter of conscious control. The resources and authority available to the managers of the E.E.A. are so great that the final result and state of the money structure when a movement has spent itself is just what they choose to make it.

CHAPTER 7

I N Chapter 4 we analysed the features of the E.E.A.'s operations and grouped them into four main phases, each phase deriving its distinction by the nature of the main action in the Exchange Market. We noted also that the classification did not exclude subsidiary operations which have been undertaken when necessary. We have not exhausted the features of the E.E.A., and we must now enquire into two further periods which are particularly instructive as they provide evidence of the evolutionary basis on which the E.E.A. rests. Further, these periods have tested the powers of the E.E.A. to offset a large volume of incoming capital and an equally large volume of outgoing capital but in much shorter space of time. It is true that throughout the history of the E.E.A. it has been called upon to deal with both sets of circumstances just mentioned, but the volume to be dealt with and the measure of time in which to do it has been such that the E.E.A. has not had its powers tested to any great extent, except for the periods we are about to consider.

The first period was from April to July 1936 and the second during May 1938. In the former period the E.E.A. was called upon to deal with a growing volume of money which left France, and to a lesser extent other countries, and sought refuge in London. Some of that money returned to France after the subsequent devaluations of the franc had taken place, but no great volume returned until after the establishment of the Daladier franc in May 1938. The nature of operations in the Exchange Market and the Money Market undertaken in 1938 were the exact opposite of those undertaken to offset the influx in 1936.

Let us deal with the first period:

When America suspended the gold standard in March 1933 there were many who considered that the remaining countries constituting the gold bloc would be forced to follow suit in a very short time. In the last respect those who thought so were quite wrong, as it was not until September 1936 that those countries did succumb, at last, to the inevitable. Before that happened however, the Governments of the countries concerned, particularly France, Holland and Switzerland, took active and severe measures to combat the forces which were undermining their ability to maintain their respective currencies on a gold basis. France, for instance, under the Laval regime, endeavoured to counter the discrepancy between the French and the world price level by thoroughgoing deflation. The gap between the two price levels was not bridged even though sterling prices, which in effect had become world prices, were beginning to rise. One of the major criticisms of the E.E.A. at that time was on account of the alleged deflationary effect its policy was having on gold prices and thus nullifying the measures being undertaken by the gold bloc countries to bring their price structure in line with that of the "sterling area". According to Professor N. F. Hall* there was a good deal of substance in that criticism, but at the moment we are not called upon to concern ourselves with this.

In France it soon became evident that although a certain amount of deflation by such means as higher taxation, cutting down of expenditure, reduction of wages, restriction of social services, etc., might have been enforced, there had to come a time when a continuance of such draconian measures was politically impossible. (That, indeed, was found to be the position in this country in 1926.) Having arrived at that point with the goal still not in sight, it was inevitable that deflation, as a policy, should be reversed. Meanwhile, many in France considered that any capital they possessed would be safer in another country, and they took steps to remove that capital to London and elsewhere. Speculators who operated on the conviction that a suspension of the gold franc was inevitable greatly increased the volume of money changing hands through the exchanges by selling the franc short. The final settlement of

* *Exchange Equalisation Account*, N. F. Hall (cf. footnote, p. 81).

these transactions involved heavy losses of gold by the Bank of France month after month. A rapidly rising crescendo of transactions and gold losses, similar to the experience of Britain in 1931, culminated in the break of the gold franc and with it the currencies of the gold bloc. During these hectic months the E.E.A. was called upon to absorb ever-increasing quantities of francs, giving pounds in exchange, and as fast as francs were accumulated they were converted to gold, "earmarked" temporarily with the Bank of France, to be shipped later to London.

In Appendix G on pp. 173-4 will be found the statistical data for this period, illustrating in figures the whole story so far as it concerned the E.E.A. and the London Money Market. In studying those figures the reader may note the small extent of the depreciation of the franc in terms of sterling during the period, relative to the considerable depreciation which occurred subsequently. It must be remembered that the franc was then on a definite gold basis and, although sterling was not, the extent of the fluctuation of the franc in terms of sterling was limited by the equation of the selling price of gold in francs and the London sterling price for gold which in turn was dependent upon other factors. Thus the range of the franc exchange rate during the period gives an inadequate idea of the volume of French money transferred to this country at that time. The conclusion that the volume was considerable may be derived from the remaining data supplied.

Here it might be useful to enquire into the possible resting places of the refugee money sent into this country. They are as follows:

1. In current or deposit accounts with banks in London.
2. In the purchase of British currency.
3. In the purchase of gold.
4. In the purchase of Treasury Bills or certain other Government securities.
5. In the purchase of securities or other assets from the public.

An authority vested with omniscient powers would be taxed to its utmost to allot the appropriate proportion of money utilised in any of the above-mentioned ways. The E.E.A. is not omniscient although it has sources of information which are exclusive to itself. In the main, indirect evidence has to be relied upon, which involves some delay in providing the appropriate action to deal with a situation requiring readjustment at any given moment. We have already observed that under the present monetary system the corrective to an import or export of gold is not automatic but must be deliberately and consciously applied. It would be a simple matter to apply the remedy if the requirements called for only one type of corrective, notwithstanding the nature of the asset acquired with the sterling transferred to French nationals. The total amount of incoming capital would be all the knowledge necessary to set in motion the secondary offsetting operations. But that is far from being the case.

Let us examine the effects of a gold purchase in London by a foreigner who has obtained a sterling deposit in exchange for, let us say, francs. Assuming that the E.E.A. was intervening at the time, the sterling obtained by the foreigner was made available indirectly by the E.E.A. which, in turn, secured sterling from the London Money Market by the sale of Treasury Bills. There is, therefore, a credit in the form of a deposit for the account of the foreigner, and a debit to the E.E.A. in the form of Treasury Bills. Now, the foreigner utilises the sterling credit in the purchase of gold, and if it is bought from the E.E.A. the credit is transferred and will serve to cancel the debit created by the E.E.A. when the funds were borrowed from the market in the first instance. In the last analysis the transaction is an exchange of gold abroad for gold in London—the sterling counterpart to each end of the transaction being incidental.

Precisely the same reasoning may be applied in the case of a purchase of Treasury Bills or certain other Government securities with foreign currency via sterling. The date of issue of Government securities acquired by owners of refugee capital determines the nature of the impact on the Money Market.*

On the other hand, if gold is bought in the open market and is not obtained from the E.E.A., the seller, in the normal course of things, will pay the proceeds he receives into his banking

* For fuller consideration of this point see Chapter 11, p. 104.

⟨ 53 ⟩

account. In this case, he, the seller, will receive the credit originally held by the foreigner and made available by the E.E.A. Before it is extinguished the credit may change hands many times; it will exist somewhere in the market just as the Treasury Bills—the debit of the E.E.A.—will be renewed and remain in the market until the original double operation is reversed and the foreigner's capital is repatriated. But until that happens the effect on the Money Market is a contraction of the cash ratio of the commercial banks because they have opened or increased a deposit and against it they have bought Treasury Bills leaving the amount of their cash unchanged. If the seller of the foreign currency chooses to utilise the sterling acquired in the purchase of stocks or shares or any other "real" asset from the public, the net effect, providing the E.E.A. supplies the sterling in the above-described manner, is a contraction of the cash ratio of the banking system.

From all the above we may establish the following principle: When foreigners acquire sterling from the E.E.A. in exchange for foreign currency and utilise that sterling in the purchase of War Loan, for instance, from an English holder who puts the money on deposit instead of buying, say, British American Tobacco Company shares, the effect is deflationary. The crucial point is the creation of a deposit out of funds provided at some time by the E.E.A. If there is no continuing deposit after the acquisition of assets by the foreigner the effect is neutral.

Of the five possible forms of assets in this country that foreigners may acquire with sterling obtained through the exchanges, there remain to be considered the complications that arise following the opening or increasing of current or deposit accounts and the acquisition of currency notes and their removal from circulation.

We have seen in the previous chapter how a current or deposit account opened on behalf of someone abroad increases banks' deposits, regarding the market as a whole, but not their cash, and in consequence their cash ratios to sight liabilities decline. We have seen also that at one stage in the cycle of operations Bankers' Deposits with the Bank of England are increased, being the proceeds of the sale of foreign currency to the E.E.A. by the commercial banks, and that they are reduced again by the operation of the E.E.A. in borrowing sterling from the market. The "proportion" of the Bank of England has not been affected by these transactions. The piling up of deposits with the commercial banks, thereby reducing their ratios, will sooner or later force the banks to call in advances or take some other deflationary step to restore their ratios. But before that happens the E.E.A. will step in with the appropriate action to restore the commercial ratios, if they do not wish any contraction in the credit base to materialise.

During the period which we are considering, the decisive action taken by the E.E.A. took the form of sales of gold to the Bank of England in large quantities. It is permissible to claim that the E.E.A. was the seller because the Bank of England's buying price for gold remains at its statutory figure.* As that price is below that which has ruled consistently in the open market since 1931, the gold could have been supplied only by the E.E.A., it being empowered to bear the book loss involved. To restore the commercial banks' ratio by sales of gold, it is encumbent upon the E.E.A. to sell an amount calculated to accomplish the purpose. As we know that the ratios of the commercial banks are of the order of 10% it follows that the amount of gold required must be in the proportion of 10:100. This, at least, is the theory. It is qualified to some extent by the fact that the 10% ratio maintained by the banking system is not wholly with the Bank of England;† it includes actual cash in the tills as well as deposits with the Bank of England; and the proportion of each item is in the knowledge only of the individual bank concerned. Some clearing banks use this margin of ratio when convenient to them. The direct action of the Bank of England on the credit structure via Bankers' Deposits is only effective fully if the till, i.e. Bankers' Deposits plus notes and coins with the clearing banks, is constant.

* See Addenda, p. 143.
† At the end of April 1938 Bankers' Deposits with the Bank of England were £113 millions, and the total deposits of the clearing banks were £2268 millions, a ratio of 4.98%.

Referring to Appendix G on p. 173 it will be noticed that the "proportion" fell to 25·5% and Bankers' Deposits to £78·2 millions, and that the corrective by gold sales was conducted on an increasing scale for some weeks. Other evidence of the strain at this time is to be seen in the high rate (in comparison with that ruling for many weeks previously) for Treasury Bills, that for the third week in June being 18s. 1d. %—an indication that considerable sums were being borrowed from the market to pay for the newly acquired foreign exchange. "Window-dressing" operations were responsible for some tightness in the market at this time, but they were not so severe as to cause this high rate for Treasury Bills. By the end of July a return to normal had been effected, and the "proportion", Bankers' Deposits and Treasury Bill rate were back to the same figures, approximately, as were shown before the period of strain commenced. The items registering at the end of the period a considerable increase over the normal are Gold Holdings and Notes Issued. Some observations on these items will be necessary, but before leaving the general outline of this period it will be an advantage to trace step by step the secondary offsetting operation of the E.E.A. in relieving the pressure on the Bank of England and the banking system.

For our purpose we shall extract the relative items (in round figures) from the weekly statement of the Bank of England at a date before the gold sales commenced, ignoring other figures in the composition of the weekly statement reflecting transactions with which we are not concerned at the moment.

BANK OF ENGLAND   15 *April* 1936

ISSUE DEPARTMENT

Notes issued:		Gold Holdings	£201 millions
In circulation	£422 millions		
In Banking Department	£40 ,,		

BANKING DEPARTMENT

Deposits:		Notes (Reserve)	£40 millions
Public	£10 millions		
Bankers	£105 ,,		
Others	£37 ,,	Proportion 26·3 %	

The transfer of French francs to London on a large scale began in the last week in April, and continued in the following weeks. Bankers' Deposits, as we have seen, declined to £78·2 millions. To correct this restricted cash basis the E.E.A. began the gold sales, and by the first week in August the Bank of England had bought at the fixed price,* approximately, £42 millions.† The item "Gold Holdings" in the Issue Department was increased by that amount and notes were issued in exchange. The notes were paid in to the Banking Department, and the funds of the E.E.A. in Public Deposits thereby increased. By these transactions, and ignoring others, the weekly statement was changed as follows:

ISSUE DEPARTMENT

Notes issued:		Gold Holdings	£243 millions
In circulation	£422 millions		
In Banking Department	£82 ,,		

BANKING DEPARTMENT

Deposits:		Notes (Reserve)	£82 millions
Public	£52 millions		
Bankers	£105 ,,		
Others	£37 ,,	Proportion 42·2 %	

So far, the Bank of England's position has been corrected, which is not enough. The additional credit obtained by the gold must be forced into the commercial banking system where it is wanted, and removed from Public Deposits where it is immobilised. As the E.E.A. has received cash for its gold it will use that cash to pay for further purchases of francs in the Exchange Market instead of borrowing, or, if no further purchases are required, it will buy back Treasury Bills from the market or will take up maturing tender bills and exchange them for tap bills, thus restoring the capital assets of the E.E.A. to their original form. The adoption of any of these methods will put cash into the market and the reflection of it will be shown in the Banking Department, where Public Deposits will decrease and Bankers' Deposits increase. The "proportion" will be unchanged

* See p. 83.
† This item, to the E.E.A., is equivalent to £67 millions assuming a market price of 135s. per fine ounce.

⟨ 57 ⟩

by the switch from Public to Bankers' Deposits, but the cash ratios of the banking system will be restored. Corrective action of this kind was undertaken simultaneously with the gold sales.

The increase in deposits, decline in the cash ratios and the contraction in the Bank of England's reserve has been offset by the simple technique employed by the E.E.A., which has released some of its gold to the Bank of England. The amount of gold disposed of in that way was decided by the general principle that the correction may be achieved by the sale of £10 gold for every £100 of abnormal deposits, the remaining £90 being already offset by sales of Treasury Bills to the market. The restoration of the commercial banks' ratio could have been accomplished by the Bank of England's purchase of the required amount of Treasury Bills from the banks, but there would have been little wisdom in the adoption of such a method at a time when those banks were in need of expanding, not contracting, their bill portfolios.* Moreover, bearing in mind future possibilities, the Bank of England's position was greatly strengthened by an increase in its gold stocks.

So much for deposits and the correction thereto. We have now to consider the question of notes.

If the reader will refer to Appendix G once again he will notice that the figures representing the note circulation show a considerable rise over the period, nearly £27 millions in four months being shown. This increase was largely responsible for the decline in the Bank of England's "proportion" until it was corrected by gold sales. The figures given are the amount of notes in actual circulation, i.e. the total amount issued from the Issue Department less the amount held in the Banking Department. The sharp rise in note circulation is to a small extent accounted for by the prosperous state of the country at that time and by holiday demands. A very large part of the increase, however, represented the notes taken by French nationals in exchange for their francs, as they preferred to hoard notes instead of depositing the money with bankers. The notes hoarded in safe deposits and the proverbial French stocking were

* Cf. p. 47.

removed from circulation. So long as they were so hoarded, they performed no useful function except to satisfy the hoarding instincts of the owners. There is no direct evidence of the exact amount of sterling notes taken by foreigners for hoarding purposes during this period, but making due allowances for other expansionary influences it is possible to make the conjecture that at the very least £15 millions of notes were so removed.

Although the acquisition of notes is perfectly legal, from the banking point of view in particular and the credit basis of the country in general such action was definitely deflationary in effect, and as that result was not desired, secondary offsetting operations were essential. The withdrawal of notes has a much greater deflationary effect than the creation of a similar amount of deposits under the present monetary regime, because the amount of notes withdrawn will reduce the actual cash of the banking system and ultimately the reserve of the Bank of England, pound for pound, while primary offsetting to deposits reduces the cash ratios of the banking system only to the extent of 10% of such deposits.

It is clear therefore that the appropriate offsetting to the potential deflation set up by the withdrawal of notes from the system must take the form of gold replacement on the classical lines of the gold standard. For every note so withdrawn the Bank of England must acquire the equivalent in gold at its statutory price and it will obtain the amount of gold required from the E.E.A. The only difference between the action of this kind taken under the present regime, and that taken under a gold standard, is the reversed order of procedure. Under a gold standard, gold must be sold to the Bank of England before the extra notes are taken out, whereas under the present regime gold is put in to take the place of notes which have been already issued. The brunt of this reversed order of things falls upon the reserve.

The £42 millions in gold acquired by the Bank of England from the E.E.A. during the period must be regarded as a corrective to the ultimate deflationary effect produced by deposits and hoarded notes. Let it be assumed that £15 millions of notes

⟨ 59 ⟩

were so removed from circulation and £10 millions were required for internal needs. The amount of gold required as the approximate corrective thereto would be £25 millions, leaving £17 millions of gold to correct the deflationary effect produced by £170 millions of additional deposits. If such an amount is the correct figure to assume, it accumulated over a period of years.

There are two possible explanations for the delay in applying the corrective—firstly, during the early years of the life of the E.E.A. the full effect of its operations, particularly in the Money Market, were not easily apparent. Time, experience and the wisdom of Professor N. F. Hall (who is rightly credited with having been the first person publicly to draw attention to the phenomenon) have brought to light the deflationary aspect of incoming capital, notwithstanding offsetting operations thereto. There is some excuse for the delay in discovering this important result when all previous experience and knowledge have produced a complacent conviction that a growing volume of imported capital must lead to an enlargement of the internal credit base. As Mr J. M. Keynes has truly remarked, it is a topsy-turvy world when it can be proved that under certain conditions precisely the opposite results may be produced.

Secondly, when the authorities became aware of the paradox that sometimes black could be proved to be white in parts, they may have hesitated to apply the remedy for fear of creating wrong conclusions at home and abroad. For instance, the acquisition of gold by the Bank of England, having the appearance of permanency, it might have been supposed that the authorities here regarded the loss of gold by France as a permanent one. The authorities must have been most unwilling to allow such an unfortunate impression to take root. By delaying their action until the real reasons were apparent to all, they turned a very awkward corner and hurt nobody's feelings. It must be emphasised that this is pure supposition, though a likely one.

To summarise, the flight of French capital to this country in the months of April, May and June 1936 had a twofold effect. On the one hand the francs exchanged for sterling produced gold, ownership of which was transferred from the Bank of France to the E.E.A. In order to pay for the gold the E.E.A. borrowed sterling by discounting Treasury Bills. The greater part of the sterling acquired by French nationals was either left on deposit or withdrawn in the form of notes. By these transactions acute stringency developed in the British banking system: the reserve of the Bank of England fell to £34·7 millions, the "proportion" to 25·5%, Bankers' Deposits to £78·2 millions, while the Treasury Bill rate rose to 18s. 1d.%, the 3 months' Bank Bill rate to 15/16% and the net note circulation by £27 millions. After allowing for the greater credit requirements warranted by the trading conditions of the time and for a slight deflationary tendency which normally develops about the end of June, these indications were eloquent of the need of some counterbalancing action if damage to the financial and economic structure of this country were to be avoided. Without counteraction, the era of the vitalising lubricant of cheap money—to the maintenance of which the Government had pledged itself—would have been brought to an end, and very probably the whole system of foreign exchange operation by the E.E.A.

On the other hand, the E.E.A. was fortunately so constituted and managed that a technique was evolved and developed to harmonise its two primary functions, i.e. to absorb the disturbing migratory capital and to neutralise and isolate the produce of such action. When the stringency developed and was made so apparent by the key indicators given above, the E.E.A. undertook the required action. The instrument to accomplish the purpose was the sale of gold to the Bank of England, pound for pound, to offset notes withdrawn and approximately one-tenth of the deposits held for foreign account and derived from E.E.A. funds. To restore the indicators to their normal levels the E.E.A. sold £41·7 millions of gold to the Bank of England, which bought it at the fixed price. (We must defer to a later chapter consideration of the mechanism employed for absorbing the difference between the price at which gold is acquired by the E.E.A. and the price at which it sells to the Bank of England.)

This relieving operation also had a twofold effect. It freed the Money Market from the stringency which had developed and it replenished the E.E.A. with sterling resources with which it could pursue further operations, if they should become necessary, without increasing the borrowing powers.

The period which we have examined provided the biggest hurdle to be surmounted by the E.E.A. since its inception, and the successful surmounting of it proved the wisdom of its authors and added another chapter to the history of financial management. The financial fabric was cushioned from the impact of the huge influx of capital and, more important, placed in a secure position to withstand any disturbance that might arise when that capital went back to the countries whence it came. In May 1938 that situation arose; it constituted the second period which we have mentioned, and will form a convenient subject for the next chapter. Meanwhile, as a fitting conclusion to this, a key to the movements following an influx of foreign capital which we have endeavoured to describe is given in the table opposite. To simplify the key we have assumed an influx of £2 millions; £1 million placed on deposit and £1 million taken in notes.

CHAPTER 8

IT was hoped that the breakdown of the gold bloc, the adjustment of currencies on a lower basis and the conclusion of the Tripartite Currency Agreement in 1936 would bring about a more settled order of things and put an end to the restlessness of a section of international capital. It became apparent very soon that this hope could not be fulfilled because the political conditions of a kind that would secure the utmost value from the realignment of currencies were not present. Migratory capital was again on the march. It moved "with a rapidity that is equalled only by the shifting trends of political confidence. In so doing it cuts clean across the accepted technique of international investment. The driving force which suddenly takes millions of hot money across the frontiers and seas is not comparative interest rates but the search for security, if only that of asylum."* Any reasonable modification of Bank Rate has no effect in deterring such movements. Indeed, experience seems to have shown that the higher the Bank Rate the greater the migration of capital.

These remarks apply particularly to France and French capital for the period commencing with the first devaluation of the franc in September 1936 up to May 1938. The franc fell from 75 to 179† to the £. When it is emphasised that considerable and costly attempts were made by the French Government at various times during that period to prevent the franc falling, some idea may be obtained of the volume of capital which must have passed through the exchanges to bring about such a great fall in value. The gold holding of the Bank of France fell during the period by the equivalent of £113 millions, an eloquent testimony of the acute financial weakness of France at that time.

---

* *Financial Times*, 17 May 1938.
† See Appendix M for highest and lowest monthly franc exchange rates since 1931.

This is hardly the place to examine the causes of each successive drop in the franc from 75 to 179 to the £; we must be content to note the resulting facts and relate the bearing of them on the London Money Market, and in particular on the E.E.A.

In the main, throughout the period, the E.E.A. was more actively engaged in selling sterling and buying gold through the prior purchase of French francs. There had been small-scale repatriations of French capital in 1936 and again in 1937 requiring the E.E.A. to operate in the reverse way, but those movements were short-lived. For two years it was almost a one-way movement of capital from France to London, followed by steadily increasing deposits of the commercial banks, rising note circulation, tender Treasury Bills issued in larger quantities swelling the banks' holdings of bills discounted, in the exact manner of and continuing from the phase described in the previous chapter. During this period the E.E.A. approached exhaustion of its sterling resources, and on two occasions it was necessary to provide it with relief, the first time by the sale of gold to the value of £65 millions to the Bank of England against a reduction in the Fiduciary Note Issue, and the second by an increase in its borrowing powers of a further £200 millions. Notwithstanding the sale of gold to the Bank of England against the Fiduciary Issue, and the sale of gold to restore the Bank's reserve as well as the cash ratios of the commercial banks (considered in the previous chapter), the gold holdings of the E.E.A. steadily increased.

In May 1938 the tide turned. The French Government under M. Daladier obtained sanction to govern by decree for a limited period. After some delay, during which the franc was subject to violent fluctuations in the Exchange Markets, the first decrees announced were those of a financial nature. The Finance Minister, M. Marchandeau, declared that the rate of 179 francs to the £ would be regarded as a maximum, below which the currency would not be permitted to depreciate. It will be remembered that under the terms of the Tripartite Currency Agreement of September 1936 the franc was devalued and allowed to fall to 105 to £1. As the expected relief to the French economy was not forthcoming by this measure of currency adjustment, further falls in the franc exchange rate were permitted with the agreement of the British and American Governments; hence the need for some emphasis that the depreciation of the franc to 179 to £1 would be the last. The Finance Minister affirmed that the Government did not intend to re-stabilise the franc on a gold basis, and added that the Government had embarked upon an operation the end of which is *de facto* stabilisation. Later that day he made the announcement that "henceforth the franc can only improve and it will do so because the Government will pursue its aim with inflexible will". On the same day the British Chancellor of the Exchequer announced that "the Government had been informed by the French Government that it did not consider that the franc could be maintained at its then level and that a lower rate was contemplated. The French Government had given assurances that it was its intention to achieve, as the eventual result of its policy, a rate corresponding to the economic position and giving to France no competitive trade advantage, and that the present downward movement would be the last. In these circumstances, after consultation with the American Government and in agreement with them, the Government had reached the conclusion that the action which was being taken by France should be regarded as not inconsistent with the Tripartite Agreement. The Agreement, in the view of all three Governments, continues with full force and effect."

These assurances of the French Government and the statement of the Chancellor of the Exchequer with its underlying implications induced a surging wave of confidence in the new franc, and, more important, a belief in the ability of the French Government to maintain it not merely by well-phrased expressions of faith but by concrete acts of a financial, economic and political nature designed to support and give it lasting stability. The new rate decided upon was such that a considerable profit was available to those in France who chose to repatriate funds sent abroad at a higher level; the rate was one that offered little or no prospect of profit to speculators by "bearing" the franc;

it was one that might be the means of giving a considerable fillip to French trade if internal prices were not allowed to rise unduly; and it was one that would produce a very large profit on the gold holding of the Bank of France, sufficient to cover the temporary advances of the Bank to the State.* In short, the franc was given a considerable under-valuation in terms of other currencies.

On the first day of the new franc there was a rush to convert sterling balances held on French account to francs. In addition to the French repatriation of capital there ensued extensive profit-taking by those who had previously sold francs "short" in the hope of making the profit which would accrue by a further devaluation—a hope and a profit now realised. The franc Exchange Market on this day and a few days following was virtually a one-way market, the only seller of francs being the French control. It has been estimated that the amount of capital transferred from London to France, being either genuine repatriations or "bear" covering, was about £80 millions. That amount was transferred in three or four days. A transfer of money of this dimension from one country to another in gold standard days would have induced a crisis of considerable magnitude with far-reaching repercussions from which very few would have escaped. On this occasion the "man in the street" was quite unaware of the crisis taking place which, if mishandled, or if the means of dealing with it were lacking, would have damaged his well-being. It was not mishandled and the means of crisis-prevention were available because the contingency had been foreseen long ago, firstly, by the establishment of the E.E.A. itself, secondly, by the sound technique developed by its managers. In the previous chapter we have examined the manner by which the E.E.A. was placed in such a position that it could not only provide the amount of capital of a size mentioned above, but also ensure that the departure of that money would not create any undue or prolonged disturbance in the Money Market. Faithfully adhering to the second principle

* A very large part of the profit on gold holdings of the Bank of France was taken by the State in November 1938.

under which the E.E.A. operates, the managers purchased only those currencies immediately convertible to gold, and in the course of the years since its establishment it has been, on balance, a buyer of foreign currencies, particularly French francs. It has therefore amassed very large amounts of gold which have been allowed to exercise no influence on the credit structure except where the E.E.A. has deliberately sold previously acquired gold to the Bank of England to function in accordance with classical gold standard principles. When, therefore, this financial cloudburst struck the Exchange and Money Markets in the first week in May 1938 and sucked up £80 millions out of the London market, it did not leave a void to be filled by a process of painful and possibly destructive deflation throughout this country. An instant conjunction of supply with the demand was made with an ease and smoothness deserving of an honourable mention on the scroll of London's financial history. It is true that some weeks elapsed before all the marks on the financial structure made by the passing of that volume of money were removed by the application of new technique. The latter was akin to the usual cleaning up of litter after the passing of a triumphant procession. This chapter will take more note of the "cleaning up of the litter" phase which was not without some complications, whereas the main operation of transferring the amount of somewhere around £80 millions was relatively simple.

The primary exchange operations were the reverse of those described in the previous chapter which dealt in a more comprehensive way with the movements resulting from the incoming capital. We must note, however, one important difference. So far as the London Foreign Exchange Market was concerned, at the time of the return of capital to France in May, the aggregate of £80 millions was made up by numerous transactions involving sales of sterling against purchases of francs and the buyer of this sterling was the Bank of England, acting as agent for the E.E.A., and the ultimate seller of the francs was the Bank of France, acting as agent for the French E.E.A. The price at which the francs were made available was decided by the French authorities, who passed on the applicable rate to the British. The important difference between this phase and the former in October 1936 was therefore the change in initiative, which passed to the French. It must not be thought from this that the French authorities had not the right or the power to decide the rate at which francs should be exchanged for sterling or vice versa at any time prior to the May repatriation. In the interim from the breakdown of the gold bloc in October 1936 to May 1938 the French authorities very frequently decided the rate at which gold would be made available to the British E.E.A. The difference lies in the two outstanding phases which we are attempting to describe, the one in which the franc was a gold franc and therefore the price at which it could be exchanged for sterling was a matter for the decision of the British authorities, and the other in which the franc had become a paper franc and the rate at which it could be exchanged for gold was a matter for the decision primarily of the French. And very largely that initiative remains with them.

The primary operations presented little difficulty. They involved the supply of a huge amount of francs—a matter of concern for the French authorities; and the withdrawing from this market of a sum of about £80 millions—a matter of concern for the British E.E.A. There was, however, a considerable amount of inconvenience arising from the large number of transactions crowded into a short time. Two days after these transactions were concluded—the recognised period for spot transactions—sterling was piled up in the E.E.A. with the Bank of England, and by the time the next weekly statement was issued the item "Public Deposits" showed a rise of £26 millions on the previous week and "Bankers' Deposits" showed a fall of £29 millions. In self-defence, and in order to replace the lost cash and provide themselves with liquid resources to meet further withdrawals, the commercial banks called in money at call, reduced short loans and advances, and thus passed some of the strain on to the short-loan market. Until this strain was relieved by offsetting operations the effect was definitely deflationary and it could not be relieved simultaneously with the operations which created the strain because under the present technical arrangements of the market it takes a certain time to get money back into the stream where it is not immobilised.

The fall in Bankers' and rise in Public Deposits of the amounts mentioned above seem small compared with the estimated amount of total withdrawals, but it must be remembered that the Bank of England's statement showing those figures appeared several days after the commencement of the movement. It must be presumed therefore that the E.E.A. had already taken steps to neutralise the flood of money going into its account with the Bank of England. The outsider cannot therefore supply exact figures covering all the money movements that took place at that time. Nevertheless, the weekly statement for several weeks following the withdrawal, and the commercial banks' weekly figures, do enable one to obtain a fairly complete story; and, fortunately, for this work, exact figures are not essential as we are more interested in the general design. If the £80 millions came out of deposits and were converted to francs there would be little difficulty in indicating the changes which would occur. They would be as follows:

BANK OF ENGLAND

| Public Deposits | ... | +£80 millions |
| Bankers' Deposits | ... | −£80 millions |

COMMERCIAL BANKS

| Deposits | ... | ... | −£80 millions |
| Cash | ... | ... | ... | −£80 millions |

EXCHANGE EQUALISATION ACCOUNT

| Gold | ... | ... | ... | −£80 millions |
| Sterling ... | ... | ... | +£80 millions |

Actual changes, however, were not quite so simply discovered, as the total amount of repatriated money was not derived solely from deposits. In the absence of exact figures which are not ascertainable we must assume the proportions of the various forms in which that money was held immediately before conversions for repatriation. Let us assume, therefore, the following:

Deposits	£35 millions
Notes	£10 ,,
Treasury Bills (or certain other Government securities)	£20 ,,
Securities (non-Government)	£15 ,,
	£80 millions

In Chapter 7 we enquired into the effects produced by the employment of foreign funds in gold, Treasury Bills and non-Government securities bought from the public. We showed that assets, such as gold or Treasury Bills* supplied by the E.E.A. and paid for out of sterling received in exchange for foreign currency at a time when the E.E.A. was one party to the transaction, neutralise or extinguish liabilities of the E.E.A. in the form of Treasury Bills to a corresponding amount. The Money Market's part in these transactions is simply that of a viaduct. It was established also that securities, other than Government, obtained from the public leave the deposit (established by the sale of currency) a continuing one, extant with the Treasury Bills (sold to the market to provide the sterling) and that the effect on the Money Market as a whole is a slight contraction as expressed by the reduced cash ratios of the commercial banks. This condition remained until secondary offsetting operations were undertaken or the series of transactions was reversed in the natural way by the repatriation of the foreign capital.

Secondary offsetting operations, as we know, were necessary to restore proper proportions, but at last the outward flow has commenced, and the transactions appropriate to them are the reverse of those described for the inflow. The liquidation of Treasury Bills by French holders involved no discomfort to the Money Market—the viaduct—and the same may be said of gold. The E.E.A. absorbed both types of assets and in so doing liquidated an equal amount of its liabilities. The £15 millions of non-Government securities which we have assumed to have been held by French interests immediately before repatriation

* See p. 53.

⟨ 70 ⟩

are in a different category; the funds used by the public in the purchase of these securities reduce deposits, and the effects produced by such reductions are precisely the same as are produced by a withdrawal of funds held on deposit.

The closing of £35 millions of deposits and the sale of £15 millions of securities have involved a transfer of similar amounts from Bankers' Deposits with the Bank of England to Public Deposits; and the dehoarding of £10 millions of notes, passing via the commercial banks, has increased the reserve of the Bank of England and reduced the note circulation. At this stage the cash ratio of the banking system has fallen because deposits and cash have declined by an equal amount. As regards the Bank of England no change has taken place in the reserve by reason of the transfer of £50 millions from Bankers' to Public Deposits, but it has been increased by the acquisition of £10 millions in notes, and the "proportion" has gone up.

Meanwhile, action should be taken by the E.E.A. with the object of returning to the market the cash withdrawn in payment for the francs, and, if the double operation can be effected concurrently, little if any disturbance in the market will be experienced. But that has not been possible, at least not to the full extent required, under the technique in practice. This may seem odd, but a remark or two will demonstrate its truth. It would seem to be a simple matter to get cash back into the market by the expedient of Treasury Bill purchases, especially as there were willing sellers of Treasury Bills in the market at the time, being French holders wishing to repatriate. But that part of pre-converted capital presented no difficulties and required no offsetting, so that sellers of Treasury Bills over and above the amount previously held on French account had to be found. It would have been undesirable to call upon the bill portfolios of the commercial banks at a time when a conjunction of forces was compelling those banks to become buyers of bills themselves for reasons unconnected with this repatriation of capital. Such forces apparent at this time were, firstly, the recession in trade bringing about a reduction in trade advances necessitating an alternative outlet for money; secondly, the approaching half year's balance-sheet requirements of the commercial banks; and lastly, the preparations for the disbursement of the War Loan dividend on 1 June. It is true that eventually Treasury Bills were obtained from the market but not as a simultaneous operation with the exchange of francs for sterling. There was therefore a time lag before the completion of the adjustment which, as we shall see, required four or five weeks.

Two expedients were immediately resorted to in the absence of the direct means of restoring the position, the object being to reduce the large amount of money locked up in Public Deposits. Firstly, £8 millions under Ways and Means advances were taken over by the E.E.A., and secondly, the E.E.A. bought Treasury Bills from the Bank of England, whose holdings of Government securities fell by a similar amount. By these means the Bank of England's "proportion" was increased, thereby giving scope for operations in the market whenever opportunity offered.* The E.E.A., on the other hand, exchanged sterling balances and acquired tap bills, the original form of its assets. The next step of the E.E.A. was to allow any of its maturing tender bills acquired from the market to be replaced by tap bills instead of renewing them in the market. In consequence the amount of Treasury Bills allotted was reduced by £5 millions, and in the following week the amount offered for tender was reduced by £15 millions, leaving those amounts of cash in the market.

A further expedient, an unusual one, was adopted to provide relief to the market subject to strain occasioned by the sudden heavy calling in of funds by the commercial banks. Those banks were endeavouring to provide themselves with money to pay for the francs they had acquired. The Bank of England made it known in the market that any discount house or bill broker finding itself hard pressed for cash at this time could sell Treasury Bills to the broker who usually acts for the Bank of England, at the prevailing rate for such bills. This was unusual, because the traditional practice, as we know it, is for discount houses and bill brokers in times of tight money to go direct to the

* See p. 105.

"lender of last resort", i.e. the Bank of England, and in that case the rate applicable is Bank Rate. As it would be manifestly unfair to penalise the discount market by charging them Bank Rate for funds, the urgent need of which arose out of conditions produced by migratory capital and not internal abnormalities, the Bank of England adopted this expedient (not without precedent) of what may be described as the "one remove"; its own well-established practice being necessarily retained, but short-circuited for the short period of the emergency. By such means the market was relieved of some of the pressure and the E.E.A. got rid of some of its surplus sterling.

If no other influences were at work, no more would be necessary than a continuation of the above-described methods of providing relief for the position to be completely adjusted. In that event the respective figures for Bankers' and Public Deposits with the Bank of England would be restored to their pre-repatriation levels. Other influences were, however, at work and they delayed the fulfilment of the complete adjustment; such, for instance, as "window-dressing" operations which commercial banks habitually undertake for balance-sheet purposes at the end of June and December. The scale on which this manipulation was carried out in 1938 was much smaller than is usually the case, because the banks, having the right to stipulate the date of maturity of the Treasury Bills they buy, have adopted the practice of so arranging their maturities of bills in June and December as will place them in funds at the times required. As a consequence the Government is forced to borrow at such times from the Bank of England for the few days when the commercial banks are not lenders. Nevertheless, some disturbance does take place for "window-dressing" purposes, and to the extent of such operations they run counter to the objective of the E.E.A. which is to relieve the stringency in the market as a whole as quickly as possible. A few words are necessary to explain this apparent anomaly. The clearing banks, when engaged upon "window-dressing" operations, created liquidity for themselves at the expense of other members of the short-loan market. This was an added strain to that caused by the repatriation of French capital which the E.E.A. was endeavouring to relieve in various ways. Normally such relief would be provided through the medium of the clearing banks, but on this occasion "window-dressing" operations would soak up such relief. Furthermore, the clearing banks not only pay particular attention to the cash ratio, but also to their "second line of reserve", which consists of cash, call money and bills, the last two items being regarded as "near cash". The ratio which these items bear to deposits has been of late about 33 %. At the end of June and December it is usual to find an increase in the bill portfolios (largely made up of Treasury Bills) and in the cash of the banks. To the extent that the clearing banks were actively engaged in acquiring bills at the time of the relieving operations following the French repatriations, the smaller was the success of the E.E.A. when attempting to pump cash into the market where the strain was being experienced. Holders of Treasury Bills (outside the clearing banks) not subject to pressure, being well aware of these competitive demands, were less inclined to sell. Their reluctance was reinforced by the extreme probability that Treasury Bills would become scarcer still as repatriations of capital continued.

Another influence dominating the market and also running counter to the needs of the E.E.A. was the necessity for the cumulation of funds in Public Deposits out of which the War Loan dividend payment of about £35 millions due on 1 June could be met. The two needs were mutually exclusive and reconcilement was not possible prior to the disbursement of the dividend. This explains the otherwise inexplicable locking up of large amounts in Public Deposits for so long a period. Reference to the table in Appendix H, giving the relative figures from the weekly statements of the Bank of England, will show that Public Deposits did not decline to the normal level until after 1 June.

Normally, the funds required to pay the June War Loan dividend are borrowed. The Floating Debt is increased either by Ways and Means advances from the Bank of England or by the issue of Treasury Bills. On this occasion the proximity of the May repatriation to the June War Loan disbursement necessitated a different arrangement. The authorities could not borrow from the market at a time when cash supplies were being drawn off by the French withdrawal. At the same time the E.E.A. was gorged with sterling and was anxious to return it to the market by some means as quickly as possible. As we know, it managed to return a portion but not enough. The opportunity to return the balance was not provided until 1 June, the date of the War Loan dividend. The two requirements were then reconciled. The E.E.A. handed over its surplus cash and received tap bills in exchange, and the Bank of England paid out the dividend. There was, in consequence, a transfer of funds from Public to Bankers' Deposits. The encashment of the dividend warrants eventually reduced the total of Bankers' Deposits, a decline counterbalanced on the other side of the Bank of England's balance-sheet by a fall in Government securities, being the reflection of the exchange of tap bills for sterling with the E.E.A. As there was no fresh borrowing for the War Loan dividend disbursement the floating debt was not increased; so that in due course, when revenue flows in at a greater rate than the outgo on expenditure, the surplus will be utilised in retiring tender Treasury Bills from the market, a retirement which would have taken place after, and in consequence of, the French capital repatriation if the War Loan payment had not made that course impossible.

Although the War Loan operations are no concern of the E.E.A. we have given them brief mention because, running counter to the offsetting operations of the E.E.A., the published figures (see Appendix H) relative to this period are unintelligible without an explanation of the cross-currents at work.

A key planned on similar lines to that facing p. 62 is given to conclude this chapter. For simplification, the movements assumed to have taken place and shown in the key take no account of the War Loan dividend payment. It must be particularly noted that the key presumes the secondary offsetting to have taken place, thus fully completing the cycle of operations beginning with the influx of foreign capital and ending with its

⟨ 75 ⟩

efflux. But those secondary offsetting operations have not been carried out and it is unlikely that they will be. Other factors having no connection with exchange operations of the E.E.A. have become active, rendering it inadvisable to allow full adjustment to be carried out. Such adjustment most probably would take the form of gold action, but this time the E.E.A. would buy gold from the Bank of England in the appropriate proportions to offset a reduction of deposits and the return of notes and thus contract the credit base.

The factor of the trade recession also accounts for the fact that the published figures of the clearing-bank averages for the period covering the return of money to France do not appear to support completely the outline of movements described in this chapter. Here are the figures:*

1938 (in £ millions)

	April	May	June
Deposits	2268·0	2262·7	2299·4
Cash	246·4	231·7	246·6
Call money	150·1	146·1	153·7
Discounts	248·5	279·6	289·4
Investments	637·7	630·6	629·6
Advances	993·7	981·0	980·5
Acceptances	111·9	116·0	116·0
Cash to deposits	10·87 %	10·22 %	10·73 %

Before remarking on these figures it will be advisable if we state briefly what we would expect to find in the published figures for a period covering a large outward flow of capital. The exchange operations only would produce:

> a fall in deposits and bank cash, and in consequence a decline in cash ratio.

E.E.A. offsetting operations only would produce:

> a fall in bills or short loans, a rise in cash and a rise in the cash ratio.

* Extracted from the *Financial Times*.

The net effect of the above operations combined would be:
deposits and bills and/or short loans decline by the same amount. As cash would be unchanged, the cash ratio to deposits is higher. This is an expansionary condition.

The above is the effect produced by withdrawals of deposits and offsetting thereto: the return of notes would increase deposits and cash and increase the cash ratio.

The actual figures for the end of May, compared with April, show a slight reduction in deposits, a greater fall in cash, a considerable increase in discounts and a distinct fall in the cash ratio. As regards the increase in discounts (bills) part of the increase must be accounted for by the decline in advances—a reflection of the trade recession. Making due allowance for factors having no connection with the special operations under examination, these figures show clearly that the E.E.A. was not able to return to the market the full amount of cash immobilised by the French withdrawals by the end of May, i.e. about four weeks later. The June figures, on the other hand, show the position completely restored as regards cash and cash ratio, and in addition provide evidence of the influence of the War Loan dividend disbursement and "window dressing". It is these influences which account for the fact that deposits and discounts are very much higher instead of being lower as we should expect.

The conflict of the published figures with the theory of the mechanism of the E.E.A. has prompted the inclusion of the above end-of-April bank figures and Bank of England figures in the key provided in the table facing p. 76, superimposing on them only those movements attributed to E.E.A. action in the amounts estimated on p. 70.

PART III

CHAPTER 9

THE reader of the foregoing chapter will have noted the important part that gold has had in the working of the E.E.A. The success or failure of the phase described therein was of paramount importance to this country; a failure would have produced dire consequences. The successful accomplishment of the set problem produced nothing spectacular to catch the eye of the ordinary man—in a way, that was a measure of its success—but it did provide a demonstration of the power and the efficiency of the managers of the E.E.A., the soundness of its concept and an object lesson. The undoubted powers and efficiency would have gone for naught but for the solid foundation provided by a sufficient quantity of gold accumulated out of past international money upheavals. The E.E.A. has acted as a buffer to the credit structure, and gold has been proved to be the nodal point.

From time to time there have been criticisms in Parliament and Press regarding the cost of financing huge quantities of gold imported to this country to be interned in vaults or held under "earmark" abroad. As regards cost, the financing of such gold now involves a charge of about $\frac{1}{2}$% per annum, the rate at which the Government can borrow on Treasury Bills.* Supposing the whole of the borrowing powers of the E.E.A. and capital assets had been converted to gold—a supposition very far from the case at present—the cost to the E.E.A. to finance £575 millions would be about £2,875,000 per annum. In fact, gold and immobilised assets together amount to about seven-tenths of the

* On this question of the cost of financing gold Sir John Simon, the Chancellor of the Exchequer, stated: "...an estimate of the maximum expense involved even if the whole of the account were continuously in use can be reached by applying the average rate for Treasury Bills which was 11s. 8d. % last year (1936). The expenses of management including the cost of handling gold are to the order of £30,000 a year." Official Report, *Parliamentary Debates*, vol. 325, 2148.

total assets, but for the sake of rebutting criticisms let the larger figure be assumed. That does not seem to be a very large insurance premium (which is the correct way of regarding it) to pay for protection against the risks that would arise by the lack of gold at such times as in May 1938 when £80 millions of "flighty" money took wing and departed in a few days. It does not require much imagination or extensive knowledge to envisage the conditions which might have been produced if the equivalent in gold had not been instantly and freely available during those critical days.

The importance of gold being held in large quantities by the E.E.A. does not rest solely upon the occasion just referred to, notwithstanding its decisiveness. Further support for the assertion may be found in the fickle moods of the "currency shy" holders of capital, who frequently discard their former preferences and find virtue only in gold, which they make unseemly haste to acquire. The E.E.A. being less, if at all, fickle, parts with gold as cheerfully as it acquired it formerly, and if, figuratively, it does so with a smile, it may not be unconnected with the probability that when the parting of gold is done, the E.E.A. is left with a substantial profit. But without gold in the E.E.A. there would have been havoc in the Exchange Markets.

Perhaps the greatest degree of importance attached to the gold assets lies in the ability they have given to the E.E.A. to maintain its purposive function of controlling the sterling exchange rate since the change in fundamental conditions brought about by the breakdown of the gold bloc—a period which we have described in chapter 4 as the fourth or gold phase. The initiative in foreign exchange operations, through events previously mentioned, has passed out of the control of the E.E.A., at least, to a very large extent, but the direct initiative lost in the Foreign Exchange Market is more than counterbalanced by the monopolistic position it has acquired in the Gold Market. It is able to absorb large quantities when they are thrown on the market—as at the time of the gold scare*—and,

* See p. 110.

〈 79 〉

if need be, to supply the considerable amounts required. If it is so minded, it can replace some of its stocks sold on the market by the absorption of the weekly arrivals of newly mined gold. Such a predominant position gives the E.E.A. absolute power to control the sterling price of gold and the respective "premium" or "discount" over or under the dollar shipping parity.* If the managers of the E.E.A. desire shipments of gold to America to take place they will allow the "premium" to fall below 1d. per ounce; on the other hand, the "premium" can be controlled to make shipments unprofitable. The importance of control over the size of the "premium" or "discount" lies in the leverage it gives to the authorities to regulate within limits the sterling-dollar exchange rate. If the "premium" is lowered to allow shipments to take place, the result produced by the sale of the gold on arrival in America is a sale of the proceeds, i.e. dollars, which will be offered in the Exchange Market against pounds, and thus affect the exchange rate. In this manner some considerable initiative lies with the managers of the E.E.A. vouchsafed to them by the distribution of the assets in such a way as to give them predominance in three directions—Gold, Exchange and Money Markets. The extent to which this control is exercised independently of the American authorities is a matter which the outsider is not able to assess precisely. There is no doubt, however, that the E.E.A. is in a position to maintain initiative, if it wishes, within the framework of the Tripartite Currency Agreement.

It is clear that gold has been the key to much of the success to which the E.E.A. may lay claim. That being so, it will be useful to enquire into the composition of its assets, particularly the amount of gold. But first a few words on the question of secrecy of the E.E.A. may be suitable here. When the E.E.A. was established it was announced in Parliament that the operations and nature of assets acquired would not be disclosed in public, and this radical departure from the usual practice in the matter of public funds was excused on the grounds that dis-

* The meanings of dollar shipping parity, "premium" and "discount" are described in Chapter 10, p. 88.

closure would defeat the objects for which the E.E.A. was set up. Criticisms on this aspect of the E.E.A. were frequent and bitter during its early life, but the Government was adamant and did not give way. Much of the criticism was based on ignorance of the nature, composition and field of operations of the E.E.A., and since one of the objects was to defeat the international speculator in his dealings in sterling, the critics were unintentionally helping the speculator although their proclaimed desire was to protect the British public and taxpayer. Nothing would have suited better the interests of the speculator than a disclosure of the method of working and the assets of the E.E.A., especially if such information disclosed a weakness—which must have been a real one in the first few months of its life when it had little gold available with which to support sterling in case of need.* Had speculators been aware of that weakness there would have developed a pressure against the pound beyond the power of the E.E.A. to control.

When, in the course of time, the E.E.A. got past the stage of adolescence and acquired an unassailable strength, the case for secrecy was considerably weakened, a fact acknowledged by the Government when it announced in 1937 that henceforth the amount of gold held by the E.E.A. would be made public twice yearly, but three months late. The first figures, published in June of that year, referred to the gold holdings as at 31 March 1937, and subsequent figures have been given out at six-monthly intervals. All students of the London financial machine and British economics must be grateful for the information thus made available, as it does shed some light where hitherto there was complete obscurity, giving an unreality to all discussion on the E.E.A. But more than that has been accomplished; by making known—what many regard as very limited information

* Sir John Simon: "...a few years ago, when the total gold resources of the country were comparatively small, the E.E.A. lost in three weeks no less than £50 millions of gold. That was followed by the loss of a further £25 millions in the succeeding eight weeks." Official Report, *Parliamentary Debates*, vol. 325 (28 June 1937).

Sir John Simon refers to the year 1933 when, according to Professor Hall, we should have supported the pound *vis-à-vis* the dollar. But it would appear that we were quite unable to do so as the E.E.A. had little or no foreign exchange available. Cf. pp. 20 and 51.

though none the less welcome—the existence of the very powerful resources in the possession of the E.E.A., the latter has gained in moral strength. If it is not quite invulnerable it is at least well equipped to withstand and defeat the onslaughts of speculators if they should ever be misguided enough to make raids against the pound.

With the official figures of gold holdings of the E.E.A. and the Bank of England now available it is possible to reconstruct the assets and liabilities of the E.E.A. with a fair degree of accuracy, if not exactitude. On the opposite page there will be found an attempt on these lines covering the periods for which official figures have been given. It is in the main self-explanatory. Some further elucidation is necessary, however, on the item of accounting losses on gold transferred to the Bank of England, and one or two other matters.

It may be asked—why losses? The explanation lies in the present statutory obligations. The Currency and Bank Notes Act 1928 confirmed the buying price (77s. 9d. per standard ounce) of gold made obligatory by the Bank Charter Act 1844, and subsequent enactments have not repealed or amended that obligation. The Gold Standard Act 1925 established the selling price (77s. 10½d. per standard ounce), but this obligation to sell was suspended by the Gold Standard (Amendment) Act 1931, and such suspension will remain in force in the absence of fresh or qualifying enactments. These obligations and suspensions are made applicable to the Issue Department of the Bank of England, which, as we know, is the department responsible for the currency of the nation and the gold backing thereto. As a consequence, the Bank of England is not empowered to pay more than 77s. 9d. per standard ounce gold. If the E.E.A. must sell gold—and we know that for four months in 1937 it was imperative that the E.E.A. should do so in order to correct a tightening of credit following the inward flow of fugitive capital and hoarding of notes—it can do so only at the fixed price, notwithstanding the fact that a much higher price was paid when the gold was acquired. This contingency was foreseen by the authorities when the E.E.A. was established. The

⟨ 82 ⟩

Finance Act 1932* has a clause governing the point; Section 25, subsection 3, states:

Whenever any gold is purchased or sold on account of the Issue Department during the existence of the Account, the amount by which the price of the gold exceeds the fixed value thereof shall, in the case of a purchase, be made good to the Issue Department from the Account and, in the case of a sale, be made good to the Account from the Issue Department.

The "fixed value" mentioned in the clause is established in a previous clause (Section 25, subsection 2 (*a*)), which specifies that 77*s*. 10½*d*. per standard ounce (equal to 84*s*. 11½*d*. approx. per fine ounce) shall be used for the purpose of a valuation before the winding up of the E.E.A. This entails a previous rectification of gold losses borne by the E.E.A., and that can be done logically only on the basis of the Bank of England statutory selling price, which is 77*s*. 10½*d*. per standard ounce. In this manner the apparent contradiction between these clauses and other enactments mentioned above is resolved.

It is clear from the clause quoted that the E.E.A. bears the loss on gold sales to the Bank of England. In 1937 we know that the Bank acquired £41·7 millions, and, as shown above, it must have done so on the basis of 84*s*. 11½*d*. per fine ounce.†

If it is assumed that the average price at which the E.E.A. purchased the gold was 135*s*. there is a difference of £24·5 millions which must be carried on the books of the E.E.A. and, as it will recoup that loss only at some unspecified time in the future when the E.E.A. is wound up, the loss is treated as a loan for accounting purposes and is therefore an immobilised asset. The recoupment of the loss is governed by a clause of the Finance Act 1932 which states that:

Immediately before the Account is wound up the amount by which the market value (as agreed between the Bank and the Treasury) of

---

* See Appendix D and Addenda p. 143.

† Sir John Simon: "...the one important point to remember is that gold which has been passed from the Account to the Issue Department of the Bank is valued at 84*s*. 11½*d*., and the excess of the market value over that figure is, in substance, an asset of the Exchange Equalisation Account." Official Report, *Parliamentary Debates*, vol. 325 (1937), 2035.

the gold then held in the Issue Department exceeds its fixed value shall be made good by the Department to the Account,

so that every time the E.E.A. makes a sale of gold to the Bank of England it immobilises its funds to the extent of about 38 % of the purchase price. With the present resources of £575 millions, and disregarding any additions thereto by jobbing profits, the E.E.A. can buy gold in the market or through the foreign exchanges and resell to the Bank of England up to a total of about £1400 millions. If the E.E.A. buys gold from the Bank to correct an over-supply of money an accounting profit will accrue (which it will retain until wound up) because the transaction will be concluded on the basis of the fixed value. But, it may be pointed out, the Bank of England's obligation to sell gold has been suspended by the Gold Standard (Amendment) Act and it would seem therefore that the E.E.A. cannot buy gold from the Bank of England without legislation specially empowering the Bank to sell at a stipulated price. But that also has been provided for in the above-quoted clause, which begins with "Whenever any gold is purchased or *sold*...", etc. It is therefore clear that at the common price of 84*s*. 11½*d*. per fine ounce the E.E.A. can buy gold from or sell gold to the Issue Department.* (Note the fact that the E.E.A. and not the public is empowered to buy gold from the Bank of England.)

The amounts of the estimated accounting losses borne by the E.E.A. are shown in the table facing p. 82, to which attention has been drawn. On the March 1938 figures these losses represent 19·26% of the total assets—a very serious depletion. Fortunately there are other facts which mitigate the position. Pursuant to its functions, the E.E.A. has bought foreign currencies and converted them to gold and it has undertaken the reverse process as well as dealing direct in the Gold Market, sometimes as a buyer and at other times as a seller. As both foreign currencies and gold in terms of sterling have fluctuated considerably during the life of the E.E.A. it follows that, in dealing in them, the E.E.A. must have incurred jobbing profits and losses. In answer to questions on the subject in Parliament,

* See Addenda p. 143.

⟨ 84 ⟩

more than once it has been announced by the Chancellor of the Exchequer that the E.E.A. continues to show a profit on its operations, and in answer to a supplementary question it has been stated by the same authority that there is a profit shown after making due allowance for the losses borne by the E.E.A. on the gold sales to the Bank of England and also "the accounting profit on revaluation at the market price of amounts thus transferred".*

These facts being established, we can take a step further than has been taken in the "Reconstruction of E.E.A. figures" facing p. 82 by stating that, although 19·26% of the assets are shown to be immobilised, there exists an amount (unascertainable but undoubtedly considerable) made up by the net jobbing profits cumulated since the E.E.A. began operations, and that amount is available for its own immediate use as and when required. Profits in this category are actual as against paper losses figuring in the accounts, which are recoverable only at the end of its life. The Finance Act 1932 has ensured that such profits may be used only for the direct purposes of the E.E.A. They cannot be applied, for instance, to make good a short-fall in budgetary revenue or for relieving taxation, as the Chancellor of the Exchequer has been invited to do on more than one occasion.

It has been claimed in some quarters that such provisions may be circumvented by applying Section 6 (1) and (2) of the Currency and Bank Notes Act 1928, which states that profits in the Issue Department arising out of the issue of Notes accrue to the Treasury, and provided the E.E.A. is not wound up, the Treasury may, if it wishes, gather unto itself all or part of the substantial jobbing profits earned by the E.E.A. and apply such money as current revenue. It is difficult to see the logic in such a claim. The Finance Act 1932 expressly stipulated that the assets of the E.E.A. shall be applied, on winding up, to the redemption of debt. To circumvent this provision by invoking a clause in a statute passed years before the E.E.A. came into existence seems to be contrary to the intentions of Parliament.

* Mr Chamberlain, Official Report, *Parliamentary Debates*, vol. 323 (1936), 1176.

Before leaving the subject of gold holdings of the E.E.A. some mention must be made of the amounts sold by the E.E.A. to the Bank of England against reductions in the Fiduciary Issue. In 1933, £15 millions were sold to the Bank to reduce the Fiduciary Issue, which had been increased to £275 millions in 1931 by Parliamentary authority. The second reduction was made in December 1936, when £65 millions were sold. These sales require special mention, because they differ very considerably from those carried through in May/July 1936 and described in Chapter 7. During the latter period we know that the gold was sold to the Bank of England to rectify a contraction of credit caused by the influx of French capital and hoarding of notes. Such gold sales produced an increase in the reserve of the Bank of England and an expansion in commercial banks' cash. The sales of £15 and £65 millions, respectively, did not produce such results. These amounts of gold were sold in exchange for securities (presumably tap Treasury Bills) which hitherto had formed part of the backing to that amount of currency notes known as the Fiduciary Issue (explained on p. 31). To the extent of £75 millions, these transactions ended in the Issue Department and produced no other result than a reduction in the Fiduciary Issue from £275 to £200 millions. The remaining £5 millions of gold sold produced the normal expansion of credit.

It is possible to assign two reasons for the last transfer of £65 millions. The primary reason must have been the need of replenishing the sterling resources of the E.E.A., which had become gorged with gold acquired from France* and other countries during the months prior to the breakdown of the gold bloc. This method of restoring the sterling resources of the E.E.A. may have been judged preferable, presumably for political reasons, to an increase in borrowing powers. Meanwhile the transfer gives the Bank an invaluable instrument of monetary technique represented by the elasticity of the Fiduciary Issue, inasmuch as a reduction from the maximum by £60

* Including £38 millions gold bought by the E.E.A. from the French authorities in part repayment of the £40 millions credit obtained from London bankers.

millions having been made it may be restored, all or in part, according to the needs that may arise. There is not the same elasticity when the Fiduciary Issue is at its maximum of £260 millions, since any increase above that figure is subject to the sanction of Parliament. When the £65 millions of gold were transferred to the Bank of England the Chancellor of the Exchequer described the measure as non-deflationary and temporary. By applying this last description to the transfer it does seem as though the authorities intended to provide some elasticity in the technique of control and to that extent reinforce the powers of the E.E.A. The Bank of England is in a happy position to ease the credit situation for internal requirements when necessary and the E.E.A. can take gold back from the Bank of England against an increase* in the Fiduciary Issue if it should ever become necessary.

* See Addenda p. 143.

CHAPTER 10

IN the previous chapter, on p. 80, we mentioned "dollar shipping parity", "premium" and "discount". In order that these terms may be properly understood we give the following short description of the Gold Market and the method of fixing the gold price. The meaning of the above terms is made clear in the context.

The price of gold in the open market is "fixed" each morning at 11 o'clock at Messrs N. M. Rothschild and Sons. When fixed, the price is immediately announced to the market. Those interested work out the amount of "premium" or "discount" there may be in the price announced for gold, and the following morning the Press make mention that gold was fixed at, for example, 140s. 10½d. per fine ounce, representing a "premium" of 1½d. over the dollar shipping parity. The price of gold is decided by the co-relation of supply with demand, and although those two factors play an important part in the decision, they do not provide the initial basis on which supply and demand operate. This point will be referred to later.

The only operative statutory price for gold in this country is that imposed on the Bank of England by the Bank Charter Act 1844, which establishes the buying price at 77s. 9d. per standard ounce (equal to approximately 84s. 10d. per fine ounce).* That price, however, is not effective (so far as the public are concerned), because it is a price considerably below that which has ruled in the open market since the gold standard was suspended in 1931, and sellers of gold very naturally go to the open market where they obtain the best price. Buyers, on the other hand, are compelled to go to the open market because the obligation laid upon the Bank of England by the Gold Standard Act 1925 to sell gold at 77s. 10½d. per standard ounce was suspended by the Gold Standard (Amendment) Act 1931.

A basis for a sterling price of gold is therefore not available

* See Addenda p. 143.

in the present statutes, but America has established by statute* a price of \$35 per ounce fine gold, without, however, returning to a fully operated gold standard. So long as a fixed dollar price is maintained it is possible to arrive at the sterling equivalent through the sterling-dollar exchange rate, and since the latter is variable, the sterling price of gold must be variable too. For example:

American price of gold per ounce $\qquad$ = \$35,
Sterling-dollar exchange rate $\qquad$ = \$5 to £1.

Therefore one ounce of gold in sterling is $\dfrac{\$35}{\$5} = £7$ per ounce.

If the sterling-dollar exchange rate moves to \$4·96⅞ to £1 the sterling gold price will be

$$\frac{\$35}{\$4\cdot96\tfrac{7}{8}} = £7.\ os.\ 11d.$$

This, however, is not the whole story, as the price of \$35 per ounce is for gold in America, and the sterling price is for gold in this country. Therefore these prices are no more than theoretical parities, and to arrive at effective parities the costs involved in shipping from one country to the other must be taken into account. To calculate the amount of dollars receivable by shipping gold from this country for sale in America, allowance must be made for brokerage, packing, insurance, freight, interest and other charges incurred in this country, and brokerage or handling charge, assaying, and the American Government's commission of ¼% must be included in the charges incurred in America to complete the sale. These charges, in all, amount to about 0·65%, equivalent to about 23 cents in the dollar price for an ounce of gold. The true parity is therefore:

$35 per ounce *less* 23 cents charges = \$34·77,†

* The statute gives the American Administration power to alter the buying price of gold on giving twenty-four hours' notice.
† At the time of the European crisis in September 1938 a very large increase in insurance rates to cover war risks reduced the parity to \$34·73½. With the passing of the crisis insurance rates were reduced but not to the former level and conditions. In October the effective parity was \$34·763.

and assuming the same sterling-dollar exchange rate mentioned above, we arrive at the following sterling prices, known in the market as the shipping parity:

$$\frac{\$34\cdot77}{4\cdot96\frac{7}{8}} = \pounds6. \ 19s. \ 11\tfrac{1}{2}d. \text{ per ounce}$$

London–New York shipping parity.

On the other hand, if gold is obtained in America and shipped to this country, the sterling received per ounce on the sale must be calculated on a different dollar base. The cost of gold obtained in America is $35 *plus* the charges incurred in shipping, which amount to 23 cents assuming a similar basis of costs as for the outward shipment. The sterling equivalent therefore becomes:

$$\frac{\$35\cdot23}{4\cdot96\frac{7}{8}} = \pounds7. \ 1s. \ 10d. \text{ per ounce}$$

New York–London shipping parity.

It is apparent from these figures that an allowance of 11d. or 11½d. per ounce must be added to or deducted from the sterling equivalent of the nominal price of $35 per ounce to arrive at the respective sterling parities according to whether gold is shipped to or from America.

It is further apparent that the effective buying and selling prices to anyone making shipment of the metal are $34·77 and $35·23 per ounce, a range equivalent to about 1s. 10½d. per ounce in terms of sterling. This indicated range must not be taken to imply that the sterling price of gold cannot fluctuate by more than 1s. 10½d. per ounce, because such a meaning would suggest the existence of a fixed mean price in sterling, and that is not the case under the present monetary regime. It means that 1s. 10½d. is the possible range of the sterling price at a given sterling-dollar rate of exchange, and as the latter is not fixed, the sterling price for gold must be variable.

There is another gold currency on which the sterling price may be based. In March 1936 the Belgian Government stabilised *de jure* the belga, which for several months previously had rested on a *de facto* basis. The belga was given a gold content of 0·150632 grammes. The buying price was fixed at belgas 6614·46 per kilogramme of fine gold and the selling price at belgas 6638·70 per kilogramme of fine gold. Reducing these prices to the equivalents for fine troy ounces and allowing one per mille for shipping charges we can arrive at the following effective parities:

Brussels–London "effective" parity
= belgas 206·69 per fine ounce,

London–Brussels effective parity
= belgas 205·55 per fine ounce.

Therefore, if the belga in London is quoted at, say, 29·36½ the shipping parity is:

$$\frac{205·55}{29·36½} = £7 \text{ per ounce}$$

London–Brussels shipping parity.

The Brussels–London shipping parity is not an effective one from an arbitrageur's point of view, because the National Bank of Belgium is empowered to release gold to Central Banks of other countries but not to private institutions or persons.

Bearing the above data in mind we can now return to the daily quotations for gold in London.

If the dollar exchange rate at the time of fixing is, for example, $4·96⅞ to £1 and the gold price is "fixed" at £6. 19s. 11½d. per ounce, we know from the above calculations that such a price is the exact sterling equivalent of the effective American buying price of gold.

On the other hand, with a belga exchange rate of 29·36½, this same sterling price of gold, viz. £6. 19s. 11½d., represents a discount of ½d. per ounce on the London–Brussels shipping parity. Therefore arbitrageurs will buy gold in London, ship it for re-sale in Brussels and make a small profit.

It is thus apparent that the dollar and belga exchange rates have to be closely watched by gold arbitrageurs, and quick calculations made by them to decide whether gold is to be bought for shipment to New York or Brussels according to the relation that the sterling gold price bears to the respective shipping parity.

In comparison with the dollar exchange the belga exchange market is a very limited one, so that only small shipments of gold can be made to and from Brussels on an arbitrage basis. The explanatory remarks which follow, therefore, will refer to the dollar exchange and arbitrage.

If the gold price is "fixed" at £7. 0s. 1d. with the same sterling-dollar exchange rate as above, the price would be said to include a "premium" of 1½d. per ounce. On the other hand, a price of £6. 19s. 10d., with the same sterling-dollar exchange rate, would represent a "discount" of 1½d. per ounce. In the latter case, obviously, it would be profitable to buy gold in the London market for shipment to America, where, on sale, the dollar equivalent of £6. 19s. 11½d. per ounce would be obtained after making proper allowances for charges.

Now, supposing the "fixing" price is £7. 1s. 10½d., with the same sterling-dollar exchange rate, the "premium" will then be 1s. 11d. per ounce, and such a "premium" would make it possible to buy in New York at $35·23 per ounce and sell in London at £7. 1s. 10½d. and, after allowing for all charges, show a profit to the arbitrageur of about ½d. per ounce. It must be understood, of course, that transactions of this nature, i.e. gold shipments *to* London, are more hazardous than those undertaken in the reverse direction, because the American price is fixed, while the sterling price is a fluctuating one, and even though the exchange transaction may be carried out simultaneously with the gold transaction in New York, there is nevertheless a considerable risk entailed by the shipment of gold from America. For this reason a "premium" of only 1s. 11d. would be too narrow to cover the risk of a fluctuating price, so that in practice a premium greater than 1s. 11d. must be shown before shipments become probable. It must be explained, however, that these remarks on gold shipments *to* London are largely theoretical. The American Treasury has stated that it will release gold to Central Banks of those countries adhering to the Tripartite Currency Agreement. Whether it will permit private arbitrageurs to take gold in large quantities for shipment to London whenever the "premium" is 1s. 11d. or over has yet to be tested. Small amounts were imported from America at the end of 1937 when the "premium" was much less than 1s. 11d. Recent history, however, has shown that gold shipments from London to New York are undertaken many times more frequently than in the opposite direction, for obvious reasons.

So long as the dollar price for gold is maintained, the "discount" on the sterling price which makes shipments to New York profitable cannot normally be very great because the shipments undertaken when the discount appears would automatically increase the demand for the metal, and, unless the authorities, i.e. the E.E.A., wished to maintain a "discount" and therefore wished to continue selling gold, the extra demand in this country induced by the profitability of shipments would bring about a correction in the price and a disappearance of the "discount".

The only occasion when a "discount" of more than the normal dimensions has appeared was in June 1937, when it was $7\frac{1}{2}d.$ per ounce. It will be remembered that in May and June 1937 very large quantities of gold were shipped from Russia and Europe to America. This gave rise to a rumour that to discourage further shipments and to act as a brake on the rise of commodity prices in America, the authorities there were contemplating a reduction in the dollar price of gold. Incredible as it may now seem, in view of subsequent events, the banks, including American, which normally undertake gold shipments to America if there is a possibility of profit, on this occasion refrained from doing so because they were uncertain of the dollar price they would receive for gold on arrival in America. Foreign-owned gold held in London and new gold from South Africa and other countries were offered to the E.E.A., which appeared to be the only effective buyer at that time. The American buying price was not effective for the above-mentioned reason. The Belgian buying price, previously mentioned, was of no benefit to arbitrageurs because the belga-sterling exchange rate and the sterling gold price did not permit profitable arbitrage. For instance, on 3 June 1937 the dollar-sterling exchange rate was $4·92½, the belga-sterling rate was 29·25½ and the sterling gold price was fixed at £7. 0s. 9d. The sterling gold price was equivalent to a discount of 4½d. per ounce on the London–New York shipping parity, and a premium of 3d. per ounce on the London–Brussels shipping parity. Shipments to Brussels were therefore impossible. The managers of the E.E.A. were unwilling to allow London to become the only place where gold could be effectively sold. As Belgium was operating a gold standard, it was anomalous to find that a non-gold standard country was, at that time, the only gold buyer. The E.E.A., therefore, utilised the power it possesses of dominating the sterling price of gold, and fixed a price which would allow arbitrage shipments to be made. Thus, on 4 June the dollar exchange was $4·93, the belga 29·26½ and the gold price £7. 0s. 5d., representing a discount of 7d. per ounce on the dollar shipping parity and a discount of 1d. per ounce on the belga shipping parity. Although a discount of 7d. per ounce gives a handsome profit to arbitrageurs on shipments to New York, such shipments were not undertaken because of the fear referred to above. But the discount of 1d. per ounce allowed profitable arbitrage shipments to Belgium. The following day the discount was 7½d. on the dollar shipping parity but only ¼d. on the belga shipping parity because the belga exchange rate moved to 20·30, reflecting the operations of the arbitrageurs who had taken gold in the London market on the previous day. Eventually the rumour was denied with sufficient firmness to kill it, and the large "discount" ran off.

It is possible for shipments to America to be undertaken on a profitable basis even when there is a small "premium", provided the authorities here are willing to release gold for shipment. That is because American banks, able to rely on their home offices for handling the transaction in New York, are thus in a position to ignore certain charges which other banks must include. It has been calculated that a "premium" of ½d. permits these banks, specially situated, to operate at a small profit.

Drawing together the main points of the above data we can establish the following principle and analogy:

The factors governing the relationship of prices of gold are three, two of which are variable. Figuratively, those factors form a triangle, thus:

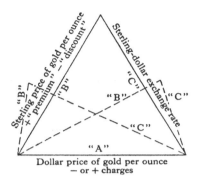

Dollar price of gold per ounce
− or + charges

The base "A" (subject only to minor fluctuations in total amount of charges) is constant, but the two remaining sides of the triangle are movable inversely with each other. If "B" is changed, and the angle narrowed then, in conformity, "C" must contract. Conversely, if "C" expands or contracts, "B" must contract or expand to conform.

The only qualification of this principle is one of degree of the contraction or expansion of the sterling price of gold, as that is cushioned by the existence of a "premium" or "discount" and thus completes that component of the triangle.

We are now in a position to answer the question: "How is the price of gold arrived at?" The basic price is that determined by the ratio of the fixed dollar price plus or minus the shipping charges and the sterling-dollar exchange rate. On this basic price supply and demand for the metal are brought into relation and the eventual price fixed is that which establishes an equilibrium between supply and demand at the time of "fixing".

If the supply or the demand is of such dimensions that the price ultimately fixed is greater than the import shipping parity or the export shipping parity, as the case may be, then forces become operative which enable a balance to be obtained in the supply and demand by a shipment of the metal to make up the deficiency in the supply or to draw off an abundance.

The E.E.A. is in a position to sell the quantities of gold required or buy those on offer and is therefore admirably placed for determining the price ultimately fixed. The E.E.A. can also determine, by the price it allows to be fixed, whether or not, gold may be bought by arbitrageurs for profitable shipment to New York or Brussels.

It will have been observed that the words "fixed", "premium" and "discount" are not used by the market in their ordinary sense.

The "fixed" price of gold is that which is arranged at the daily meeting of those concerned at Messrs N. M. Rothschild and Sons, and the expression used suggests that the arranged price is operative throughout the day. In fact, that is not so. The "fixed" price is intended to be applied to the amounts of gold changing hands at the "fixing", but gold transactions take place subsequent to the meeting and outside the premises of Messrs N. M. Rothschild and Sons. If the sterling-dollar exchange rate does not move it is possible that gold transactions done in the afternoon may be arranged on the basis of the "fixed" price, but if there is a change in the exchange rate, then the gold price at which business is done will conform to the new rate, although the same "premium" or "discount" contained in the "fixed" price may be maintained.

The words "premium" and "discount" are the terms applied by the market to indicate the margins in the sterling price of gold over or under, respectively, the price at which gold is in exact export parity with the dollar or belga price, as the case may be. Those terms do not appear to have been wisely chosen, as the layman might quite easily interpret meanings to such expressions which are quite different from those intended by the market.

For instance, such terms imply the existence of only one constant. That is not the case. We know that there is a constant for calculating the London–New York shipping parity which is $34·77, but there is another constant for calculating the New York–London shipping parity which is $35·23. The "premium" or "discount" in the sterling price for gold is always calculated on the constant applicable to the London–New York shipping parity notwithstanding the fact that the upper constant for inward shipments is the appropriate one.

It is because of this confusion in constants that, in the example quoted above, it was shown that the "premium" has to rise until it equals at least the sterling range, i.e. 1s. 10½d. or 1s. 11d., before inward shipments become profitable.

CHAPTER 11

IN the "Attempted Reconstruction of Official Figures of the E.E.A." facing p. 82 there is given the proportion which gold and other assets bear to total assets. Of these the amounts of liquid resources available at March and September 1937 and March 1938 are shown as 22·53 %, 31·99 % and 28·72 % respectively. Liquid resources must be composed of Treasury Bills, sterling and foreign currencies, if any. When the official figures were made public it was stated on each occasion that the amount of foreign currencies held was inconsiderable. Although no statement concerning holdings of sterling has been forthcoming it is fair to assume that the E.E.A. would not leave sterling balances greater than unimportant amounts immobilised in Public Deposits if it could be avoided. It would invest them in Treasury Bills in accordance with the practice followed by other Government departments.

The nature of liquid resources available must be, therefore, very largely Treasury Bills, either tap or tender. At the commencement of the cycle of operations which the E.E.A. sets in motion when it intervenes in the Exchange Market and sells sterling to prevent an unwanted appreciation or over-valuation, it is in possession of tap bills—the form of its original working capital. They are then converted to sterling either by selling them to the Bank of England or some Government department for cash, or by an increase in the tender issue of bills; usually by the last means, this being the quickest way to draw off refugee funds. For the whole period of tenancy in this country of those foreign-owned funds, there will exist in the market a corresponding amount of tender Treasury Bills, or tap bills in the Bank of England or a Government department. With the return of foreign-owned capital to its own domicile there will commence the second half of the cycle of operations, the inverse of those following an inward movement of capital, and in reverse order.

The penultimate stage should find the E.E.A. in possession of the tender bills which have been bought from the market. These will be converted to tap bills of such maturities as are convenient, thus completing the cycle.

It follows, therefore, that the E.E.A.'s liquid resources *may* be income-earning tender Treasury Bills, but for the most part they are simply rights to issue tap bills which must be brought to life by discounting before they can perform any function. Immediately before winding up, and after the disposal of gold holdings, the E.E.A. will find itself in possession of tap bill rights being the total of its borrowing powers, plus securities representing profit on exchange and/or gold holdings. The former will be extinguished by Parliament, while the latter will be applied to redemption of debt. Thus, in this matter, the essential difference between the E.E.A. and other Public departments is this—the latter have free sterling available with which they buy tap bills, while the E.E.A., commencing with no cash at all, must dispose of tap bills to obtain cash. The E.E.A. must sell bills before it can function, while the Public departments are buyers. These respective aspects are not necessarily complementary, because the E.E.A. must sell bills *in the market* if it is to offset successfully and quickly, leaving the free funds of the departments to be dealt with in the normal way and as though the E.E.A. did not exist. The E.E.A. is a buyer of bills (apart from the reclaiming of its own liabilities) only when it acquires sterling by its jobbing profits. Generally, when it acquires sterling by the sale of gold it reduces its liabilities (tender bills) in the market which were set up when the gold was bought. Exceptionally, it will postpone conversion to tap bills, if it is considered desirable to conceal operations.

The floating debt of the country, in which is included the *total* amount of borrowing power in the form of tap bills authorised to the E.E.A., does not reflect the changing character of assets held by the E.E.A. Although a decline in that part of the floating debt listed as tap bills and an increase in that part listed as tender bills may be expected to follow an influx of foreign-owned money, and reverse reflections in the case of an efflux, the total of floating debt is undisturbed by such movements. That part of the floating debt which is allotted to the E.E.A. therefore must be represented by assets in the form of gold, foreign currencies, pounds, or *unexercised means of borrowing*.

This may seem to be a cumbersome method of providing the E.E.A. with active instruments without which it could not function. The explanation is to be found in the original concept of the E.E.A. in which secrecy was an essential part. Secrecy, especially in the matter of contemporary operations, is still a valuable asset to be preserved. If the floating debt is permitted to reflect, for instance, the exact amount of Treasury Bills disposed of in the market or to Public departments when offsetting an influx of foreign capital, the task of the speculator on the search for information regarding the E.E.A. will be very much easier, and that of the E.E.A. doubly difficult. Likewise, when offsetting an efflux of capital, the E.E.A. may adopt devious means of concealing its operations. For instance, in order to avoid the indirect divulgence of information which would follow from an approximation of the published tap bill figures to E.E.A. activities, the E.E.A. may postpone to a more convenient day the exchange into tap bills which it would normally do to complete the cycle of operations. Instead it may apply for tender Treasury Bills at the weekly allotment and obtain them. It must be remembered however that, if the E.E.A. adopts this method of concealment, it will be competing with the market for the limited allotment of bills. As a consequence the market may find itself starved of those "quick assets" which are vital to the banking system. An increase in the tender bill allotment does not meet this objection—to do so would be a contradiction. If it is necessary to extend concealment beyond what is possible by the limited method of tender bill applications, no doubt the authorities will adopt other measures, of which there are many, to attain their object.

Incidentally, since the Bank of England manages the Issue Department (which is in fact, if not in name, a Government department) and the E.E.A., the powers of the Bank of England for controlling the credit situation have been enormously increased by the creation of the E.E.A., but such power would have been nullified if its operations had been betrayed by the publication of Treasury Bill figures reflecting *pari-passu* activities of the E.E.A.

It will be readily understood from the foregoing that a study of the weekly allotments of tender Treasury Bills must yield useful indirect evidence of the volume of activities of the E.E.A., subject to the qualification mentioned above. It is obvious that the E.E.A. must discount Treasury Bills to offset an influx of capital, and in order to do so the allotment must increase or the amount allotted in any particular week must exceed the maturities for that week. In either case cash is drawn off from the market. To offset an outward movement of capital the allotment each week will be decreased and bills maturing will be allowed to run off. Under-allotments* and reduced offerings for tender leave cash in the market and, like increased allotments, are cumulative in effect. For instance, £1 million of Treasury Bills under-allotted in any particular week, with subsequent allotments continued at the reduced level, result in an increase in the market's cash to the extent of £13 millions, since Treasury Bills have a life of 13 weeks. In the same way increased allotments maintained will draw off cash cumulatively until 13 times the amount of the increase is withdrawn.

It is unwise therefore for the student of the activities of the E.E.A. or of the Money Market to ignore the weekly allotments of Treasury Bills and the interplay of the amounts of new bills on maturities. It will be an advantage, too, if a study is made of the average amounts of total tender bills in issue, it being borne in mind that such issues are not made exclusively for the purposes of the E.E.A. The Government must borrow money in the earlier months of the financial year to pay for expenditure more evenly distributed over the whole year and recoup itself in the latter months when revenue overtakes expenditure. Some part of the borrowing needs of the Government will be satisfied by the Public departments, such as the Post Office, Unemploy-

---

* This manœuvre is referred to in the market as "cutting the top off" allotments—as was done on 6 May 1938 and four times during the crisis in September 1938. See Appendices H and I.

ment Insurance Fund, National Health Insurance and the National Debt Commissioners, which have funds available for investment on short and medium term. In addition, some of these departments have capital funds semi-permanently invested which provide income estimated at about £80 millions a year. From these sources there is a supply of money which is not inconsiderable but is, nevertheless, insufficient for the purpose of financing Government expenditure during the lean months, especially when the outgo approaches the rate of nearly £1000 millions per annum. As a consequence, resort must be had to the market for the necessary funds, and the instrument used for the purpose is the tender Treasury Bill. There must be, then, some relation between the weekly figures of short-fall in revenue under expenditure and the amount of Treasury Bills placed in the market for this purpose, and as such revenue and expenditure figures are regularly published it is but a short step to estimate the balance of bills in issue for other purposes, one of which must be the financing of gold or foreign exchange by the E.E.A.

It would seem, therefore, that the average amount of tender bills outstanding over a long period should bear some relation to the accumulation or depletion of gold and foreign exchange by the E.E.A. But the facts are quite different. At the end of March 1938 the E.E.A. had 42·54 million ounces of gold, and assuming an average purchase price of 135s. per ounce, the E.E.A. must have expended £287 millions, to which must be added the amount of loss borne by the E.E.A. on its gold sales to the Bank of England, estimated at £111 millions. Of these gold sales £75 millions were against reductions in the Fiduciary Issue and the assets surrendered by the Issue Department for that gold were securities, not cash. These items make a total of £473 millions, against which must be set an unknown amount made up of tap bills* in the hands of the E.E.A., representing its jobbing profits since commencement.

* It is advisable to point out here that there are two kinds of tap bills which the E.E.A. may hold. Tap bills forming its original working capital are issued or discounted by the E.E.A. to obtain cash. Tap bills acquired with free sterling at the disposal of the E.E.A. may have their origin in some other Government department. In the first case the E.E.A. utilises tap bills as a borrower, in the second as a lender. Cf. p. 99.

At the end of June 1932 (about the time when the E.E.A. was inaugurated) the total tender issue of Treasury Bills was £515 millions and at the end of March 1938 the figure was £512 millions—a small decrease, despite the fact that in the period the E.E.A. borrowed, somewhere, £473 millions. Before we seek the discrepancy, the figure for March 1938 Treasury Bills must be qualified. That date coincides with the end of the financial year, and any surplus of revenue over expenditure is automatically applied to the reduction of the amount of bills in issue. For the year ended March 1938 there was a revenue surplus of £38 millions, which we must add to that given above. There is, then, a difference of £35 millions in the amount in issue when the E.E.A. commenced operations and that outstanding in March 1938, allowing for the revenue surplus.

The answer to this anomaly is—funding operations and rearmament. The great War Loan conversion from a 5% to 3½% basis was the beginning of a long series of conversions and funding operations undertaken for the purposes of reducing the annual interest charge and funding a mass of floating debt at opportune moments. The cheapest form of borrowing, i.e. by Treasury Bills, is availed of up to the fullest limit of prudence as considered by the Treasury authorities, who endeavour to strike a balance between the claims of the taxpayer—who is very materially affected—and their own canons of sound finance. It would seem that when the total of Treasury Bills outstanding exceeds £900 millions the Treasury watchdogs become restive and steps are taken to reduce the amount by converting to medium or long term bonds. Over the period bracketed by the above-mentioned dates the net new issues of bonds less budget surpluses to 1937 amounted to £360 millions, including that portion (£35 millions) of the National Defence Loan issued in 1937 unexpended on its designated purpose. This longer term form of borrowing has replaced a similar amount on short term by Treasury Bills, by which means the E.E.A. has raised £473 millions. Some part of the gap (£113 millions) in these amounts must be made up by the jobbing profits earned during its life. We are unable to be more precise on the last point beyond stating that they are considerable. If a balance remained to be covered it is probable that the E.E.A. obtained the money by surrendering for cash to other Public departments all or part of the Fiduciary securities obtained from the Bank of England in exchange for gold. In that way, £75 millions may have been obtained.

Thus *it would appear* that the commitment of the E.E.A. to the extent of £473 millions (made up in the above-described manner) has been obtained by the issue of £35 millions additional tender Treasury Bills, £360 millions net issue of bonds, £x millions from the Public departments and £x millions jobbing profits. If it be true that three-quarters of the money expended by the E.E.A. has been financed by the expensive form of bond issues, then we must qualify the remarks on p. 78, wherein the low cost of borrowing by Treasury Bills for the E.E.A. requirements was emphasised. In fact, that assertion cannot be made, on two counts. Firstly, the funding operations and borrowing for defence requirements would have been carried out even if the E.E.A. had not existed. Secondly, the E.E.A. is financed by bonds only to the extent that owners of refugee capital invest sterling in bonds issued by the Government during the life of the E.E.A. In this case bonds have been given in exchange for gold, and the additional cost of financing such gold is a saving *pro tanto* to other Public departments.

Here it is necessary to refer back to Chapters 7 and 8, wherein considerations were given to the appropriate offsetting operations to the different types of assets acquired by owners of incoming capital. On p. 53 it is stated: "The date of issue of Government securities acquired by owners of refugee capital determines the nature of the impact on the Money Market"; this requires further elucidation.

It is obvious that the employment of such capital in Treasury Bills completes the circle of transactions and no further regulatory actions are necessary. On repatriation the circle will again be completed by the extinction of the Treasury Bill counterpart. We must, however, go further and state that this reasoning cannot be confined to Treasury Bills, but applies equally to certain other classes of Government securities. The nature of the latter is indicated by the figures given above as those relating to the different types of borrowing instruments used during the enclosed period. The portions of the Funding Loan, National Defence Loan and Treasury Bonds purchased by owners of sterling acquired from the E.E.A. by an exchange of gold must be classed with the Treasury Bills acquired in a similar manner. Treasury Bills and Bonds of that nature complete the circle; they do not disturb domestic credit and therefore require no offsetting. The purchases of Government stocks issued before the existence of the E.E.A. by owners of sterling acquired from the E.E.A. are in a different category and must be offset in a manner similar to that undertaken to offset deposits, as otherwise the net effect is a contraction of the cash ratios of the banking system.

All this is but one indication of the skill required in determining the ultimate resting places of refugee capital. It would seem that the managers of the E.E.A. are having regard for the interests of the country if they take into account the fact that for reasons unconnected with the E.E.A. some part of the liabilities set up against its gold assets are in the form of long-term instruments, and these must play a part in the offsetting operations it undertakes when repatriation is in progress. The loss of gold by the E.E.A. following repatriation of foreign capital must be replaced by other assets: sterling, Treasury Bills *and* bonds of the nature specified above and in the appropriate proportions. The bonds it acquires are held until an opportunity arises to exchange them for tap bills with the Public departments. The fall in Government securities held by the Bank of England following the May 1938 repatriation suggests that operations of this nature were in progress. The Bank of England probably short-circuited the procedure by selling £22 millions of tap bills to the E.E.A. and replaced them, after the War Loan dividend disbursement, by bonds acquired by open-market operations on behalf of Public departments.

Returning to the methods of financing the E.E.A., it is evident that, if there had been no need for funding or defence loan

⟨ 105 ⟩

operations, the increase in the total of outstanding tender Treasury Bills during the life of the E.E.A. would correspond in some measure with the amount expended by the E.E.A. in acquiring gold or financing losses on gold transfers. Alternatively, if the E.E.A. did not exist, the total floating debt would be smaller by nearly £600 millions. The Chancellor of the Exchequer in his budget speech to the House of Commons on 27 May 1938 said: "There has been an increase of nearly £600 millions (in the total deadweight debt) but nearly the whole of the difference of £550 millions was due to the Exchange Equalisation Account. It might be correct to speak of the deadweight debt having increased but it was a relevant circumstance if the increase or nearly all of it was supported by assets. The E.E.A. had assets and was making a profit. That was not the same thing as an addition to borrowing with nothing to show for it."

So we are able to state definitely that the E.E.A. is financed up to the amount of its commitments by Treasury Bills—tap and tender—less the amount invested in specified bonds, the initiative in which lies outside the control of the E.E.A.

The finance aspect of the assets of the E.E.A. provoked Mr J. M. Keynes to attempt to shatter the comfortable complacency of those who thought that the E.E.A. was, in fact, pursuing its tertiary object, i.e. to offset "hot money" so as to leave the credit basis undisturbed. He made the statement[*] that in 1937 the gold inflow, amounting to about £190 millions, was financed at the expense of the supply of domestic credit and that as a consequence gilt-edged securities had to fall sufficiently to induce holders of liquid resources to become holders of less liquid assets. He asserted that of the £190 millions of gold acquired, £104 millions was paid for by the National Defence Bonds and Funding Loan, the balance by Treasury Bill repayments and by funds from the Public departments. This, he suggests, has a deflationary effect which is undesirable.

It is difficult for the ordinary person to share that view. There are several reasons unconnected with the E.E.A. or its methods

[*] In a speech to Shareholders at Annual General Meeting, National Life Assurance Society, 24 February 1938.

of finance which would account for the fall in gilt-edged securities at that time, but as they are quite irrelevant to present considerations they need not be stated here. As for the suggestion that the cash basis was restricted, there does not appear to be much evidence to substantiate the claim. On the contrary, the usual indices point to an opposite conclusion. If we examine the figures for the year ended June 1938, a period more favourable to the assertions of Mr Keynes because for eleven months of the period gold continued to flow in at an accelerated rate, we shall find the clearing banks' cash increased by 6·7%. Bankers' Deposits and Government securities in the Bank of England also increased. The abundance of cash, more often than not, has exercised the ingenuity of those in control of institutions forming the Money Market in finding suitable outlets. These facts suggest that a deliberate effort was made to maintain a plentiful supply of cash. If credit was not utilised to the extent permitted by the cash basis it does not seem very logical to assign the fault to the E.E.A. and its activities.

This chapter set out to examine the nature of the liquid resources of the E.E.A. We have seen that this item must be made up by tender and tap bills, the latter in issued and unissued forms. For short periods it is possible that the E.E.A. holds longer-term Government securities awaiting suitable opportunities of exchange for tap bills, either with the Bank of England or any of the Public departments. The fact that owners of refugee capital may acquire newly created Government bonds is incidental. It does not detract from the main fact, which is, that the E.E.A. relies on the Treasury Bill as the instrument for borrowing operations.

CHAPTER 12

THIS work would not be complete without some further reference to the question of gold. We have examined that subject as one of the holding assets of the E.E.A. and from the point of view of the importance of gold in enabling the E.E.A. to carry out its functions. We must widen the scope so as to include considerations of other gold holdings in this country, the volatility of gold and the direct bearing this feature has had on the activities of the E.E.A.

In Appendix J the figures are given relating to imports and exports of gold since September 1931, and the distribution of the net import. Sterling values and percentages are added to the figures representing distribution, and this part of the table is worked out to show the position as at the dates on which official figures of gold holdings have been supplied, viz. March and September 1937 and March and September 1938. To facilitate reference hereinafter we shall refer to the accounting periods, to which the official figures apply, as follows: First Period—June 1932 to 31 March 1937; Second Period—1 April to 30 September 1937; Third Period—1 October 1937 to 31 March 1938; Fourth Period—1 April to 30 September 1938. From September 1931, when Britain left the gold standard, to the end of the Fourth Period, there was a net import of gold of 105·49 million ounces, or assuming a price of £7 per ounce, £738·4 millions. To this figure must be added the estimated amount of coins and old gold dehoarded in this country during the period, and there must be deducted the estimated quantity of gold consumed by industry and the arts.

We have estimated that the total of coin and the old gold dehoarded, less the quantity used by industry and the arts, is 3·5 million ounces, or in value £24·5 millions. There is therefore a disposable surplus of £762·9 millions. In our table we have assigned the appropriate amounts under the headings "The Bank

of England", "The E.E.A." and "Unaccounted Difference".*
The last heading must be understood to embrace that amount
which cannot be included in either the Bank of England or E.E.A.
holdings, as the figures for these are accurately ascertainable.
"Unaccounted Difference" gold embraces the holdings of foreign
Central Banks "earmarked" by the Bank of England, gold deposited here for safe-keeping by foreign owners, and holdings of
British nationals who individually may not legally retain more
than the equivalent of £10,000. In the First Period the Bank of
England gold holdings record an increase of £286·7 millions
and only £21 millions in the Second Period. There is no further
change in the Third and Fourth Periods. The E.E.A. acquired
£186·6 millions in the First Period, £92·3 millions in the Second,
£18·8 millions in the Third, but sold £146 millions in the Fourth
Period. On the other hand, the figures representing "Unaccounted
Difference" for the First Period were £223·9 millions, and
for the remaining periods a fall of £68·6 millions, a rise of
£12·81 millions and a further rise of £135·31 millions,
respectively, were recorded.

The recital of these changes emphasises the volatility of gold,
the brunt of which must fall upon the E.E.A., as the Bank of
England is not a free agent in the matter.

It may be useful to enquire into the causes of the change of
ownership in such a short time, as indicated by the above
figures. For the greater part of the year 1937 the French franc
was subject to pressure, and at recurrent periods required direct
support, the extent of which may be gauged by the net amount
of gold imported to Britain from France during the year, which
was £108 millions. In March and April of that year Russia
shipped considerable quantities for sale in this country. In all
about £40 millions were disposed of, which ultimately—
together with other amounts from this country and the Con-
tinent—was shipped to America. The westward flow gave rise
to a rumour that America was considering the lowering of the
price of gold to discourage further shipments of the metal.
At first the rumour was not specifically contradicted. In con-

* See footnote to Appendix J, facing p. 178.

sequence shipments to America ceased for a time and conditions amounting almost to panic ensued in the London Gold Market. The E.E.A., which earlier in the year was called upon to absorb large amounts of gold from France and to act as a viaduct for the Russian gold, was deluged with further sums from panicky holders who had previously hoarded it in this country. In one day—4 June—£4·25 millions were disposed of at the "fixing". Eventually the Washington authorities denied any intention to change the price or to adopt any device having the same effect. On 28 June the borrowing powers of the E.E.A. were increased by £200 millions, which did much to allay the panic and restore more normal conditions. Thus ended the "gold scare".*

The formation of the Chautemps Government in France, and the decision to allow the franc to find its own level, improved the prospects of that currency for a time. Some three milliards of francs returned to France in the form of gold, and it is probable that most of this was provided by the British E.E.A. This movement was soon reversed, however. Capital again left France and continued to do so up to the time of the establishment of the Daladier franc in May 1938.

Towards the end of 1937 rumour, which has no domicile nor allegiance, was again very active. This time resourceful minds suggested that the price of $35 for an ounce of gold was not inviolate. Although only a few months earlier the suggestion was made that a reduction in that price might take place, in November rumour unblushingly and inconsequently suggested that an increase in the price to $41·34 per ounce was a distinct possibility. Such was the remedy put forward as the panacea for the economic troubles that were worrying the people of America at that time. Incredible as it may seem in retrospect, this rumour took a firm hold and was acted upon. "Hot money" tumbled over itself to get out of dollars and into gold. Dollars were offered in the Exchange Markets and the "premium" in the sterling gold price rose at one time to the point at which arbitrage shipments of gold from America were profitable.† This was a complete *volte-face* to the position obtaining in the

* Cf. p. 79.   † Cf. p. 92.

previous June when dollars were heavily bought and a "discount"* of 7½d. appeared in the sterling gold price. Eventually this rumour went the way of the others, and the "dollar scare" came to an end.

During the first quarter of 1938 the attention of the financial world was focused upon the conditions in France, which steadily deteriorated. France lost much gold during this period and the E.E.A. was very active in the Exchange Market, working on behalf of the French authorities, who made valiant but costly efforts to protect the franc. The support to that currency expressed itself in large gold transfers to the British E.E.A. The culmination of these events concerning France did not occur within the periods under consideration. That has been considered in another chapter.† It is sufficient here to state that in May 1938 there was the loss of gold estimated at about £80 millions, being the counterpart to the French repatriation of capital. That was followed by a movement into gold which commenced about the end of June and assumed very large proportions in July, August and September. The buying of gold in July and August had its origin in two motives. The first can be attributed to rumours which, on this occasion, suggested that the initial Powers of the Tripartite Currency Agreement were contemplating a general devaluation of their respective currencies, or, in other words, an increase in the price of gold. The benefits to be obtained by this extraordinary manœuvre were not clearly stated. That is not surprising, as it is a little difficult to see any advantage to the Powers in the adoption of this proposal.‡ Those who believed in the rumours hastened to acquire gold for hoarding purposes.

The other motive had the merit of sound reasoning, and the gold buying following it did, at least, have an intelligent basis. The motive was the very belated recognition that sterling in terms of dollars was much over-valued. The large fall in American

---

* Cf. p. 93.   † Cf. Chapter 8, p. 66.
‡ "Taking all countries together, at a single moment of time, the result of an all-round cut in rates of exchange would resemble what follows from an all-round cut of wage costs; everyone is in the same relative position as before." Professor T. E. Gregory, *The Problem of Monetary Stabilisation.*

prices, compared with a very much smaller fall in British prices —which began in 1937 and continued in 1938—expressed itself in the trade statistics of each country. The growing adverse trade balance of Britain and the very favourable trade balance of America compelled some cognisance being given to the exchange rate of the pound, which was again out of alignment with the internal economic position. It is possible that the rapid rearmament of this country was responsible for a large part of the greatly increased imports. And a cheap dollar helps to lessen the cost of those imported materials required for armament purposes. As long as this country was a net receiver of funds on capital account—a position it occupied up to the French repatriation in May 1938—the over-valuation of the pound in terms of dollars was tolerable. A sustained reverse flow of refugee capital funds would disclose the dangerous level at which the pound was poised. The consequences which followed an over-valuation of the pound in the years immediately before the suspension of the gold standard in 1931 are too vividly remembered to allow complacency in the matter to take hold.

The negotiations for an Anglo-American Trade Agreement had some bearing on the matter. An agreement on fiscal matters would be most hazardous for this country if it were based on the maintenance of an exchange rate of the £ which was demonstrably over-valued in terms of dollars. The danger of that position is emphasised by the establishment of the Daladier franc at a level which clearly under-valued that currency, and the converse of that is over-valuation of the pound in terms of the franc. An over-valuation of the pound in terms of the two principal foreign currencies* is a matter which places some strain on the Tripartite Currency Agreement. The aspirations of that Agreement are being realised only so long as Britain is willing to accept some damage to her economic and financial position resulting from an over-valued pound. A temporary acquiescence to that inferior position may be expedient for

* Norman Crump in the *Financial Times*, 1 September 1938, estimates the pound's over-valuation in terms of the dollar as 15 % and in terms of the franc as 30 %. He points out that quantitatively these percentages may be incorrect, but the direction of currency values is unmistakable.

various reasons, some of which have been mentioned, but to establish it permanently could not have been intended when the Currency Agreement was concluded. In that Agreement competitive currency depreciation was eschewed in definite terms: the obverse of that is just as important, though not expressed. It is not surprising, therefore, that the authorities were not stubborn in maintaining the rate within a range of 5 cents either side of $5·00, a range maintained for so long that it had come to be regarded as sacrosanct. It appeared that they were not unwilling to allow the pound to find a more natural level.

Undoubtedly these considerations were in the minds of those who were actuated to buy gold or dollars—very nearly the same thing. The E.E.A. of course stood up to these demands for gold, notwithstanding the motives behind them. It did, however, try to discriminate. At the beginning of the movement the demand sprang from the first motive mentioned above—for hoarding purposes. The authorities could not have wished to facilitate hoarders and therefore they allowed the interplay of supply and demand to express itself in the size of the "premium" in the sterling price for gold. This was effective in reducing the demands for gold for hoarding purposes, but the continuing demand for gold arising out of the second motive was provided willingly and at a price which rendered some support for sterling. By fixing the sterling price for gold at $\frac{1}{2}d$. premium or even at the dollar shipping parity the authorities enabled the usual constituents of the market to take gold for shipment to America and make a small profit on the transaction. In normal circumstances, gold arbitraged in that way performs its classical function. The currency of the country exporting the gold comes into demand and the currency of the country importing the same gold is offered. The interplay of the supply of one currency and the demand for the other changes the ratio they bear to each other as expressed in the exchange rate.

Exceptional circumstances have brought about a change or a modification in this classical procedure. The demands for gold which have been made since May 1938 arose out of a variety of motives, some of which were inconsequential and others fundamental. They must be classified as exceptional. That part of the demand for the metal which had its origin in fundamental economics did not produce, to its full extent, such support for sterling as would normally accrue, because the gold or the produce of it in dollars obtained by the original buyers was retained by them until all or part of the correction to the over-valuation of sterling was realised. The E.E.A., in fixing the price of gold at one which permitted profitable arbitrage, carried out its part of the Tripartite Currency Agreement. It also pursued its primary function, that of "ironing out" fluctuations. It did not, however, oppose a definite trend, which would be contrary to the policy as laid down by Parliament originally. This situation was therefore somewhat paradoxical, for this reason. As all the gold it released for arbitrage purposes was not used, for the reason just explained, to provide support for sterling by the sale of dollars—being the produce of gold—the E.E.A. intervened in the Exchange Market and provided the required support for sterling by selling dollars. Such selling delayed, if it did not altogether prevent, the realisation of a sterling-dollar exchange rate which would be generally considered as the proper equilibrium rate between the two currencies. The inevitable establishment, sooner or later, of a truer equilibrium rate was the motive behind much of the gold buying; and the delay in the accomplishment of such a rate increased the demands for the metal or alternately prevented the development of support for sterling by natural means. The direct support for sterling by sales of dollars by the E.E.A. did not have such a decisive effect as would have been produced under more normal circumstances, because the gold counterpart to the dollar sales did not deflate the cash basis here or inflate the cash basis in America,* at least not sufficiently to provide any corrective to the dollar under-valuation.

This direct intervention by the E.E.A. in the Exchange Market implies a loss of control to some extent over the exchange rate by means of the manipulation of the size of the "premium" in the sterling gold price. At the time of writing the over-valuation of sterling has been corrected by 3 % only, so that in the absence

* See footnote, p. 139.

of an appreciable rise in the American price level by inflationary spending or other means, without a corresponding rise in the British price level, the pressure against sterling may continue.

As the rate of exchange approached the old parity of $4·86⅔, the selling of dollars by the E.E.A. was heavy, from which fact it was deduced that the authorities had no intention of allowing sterling to fall below the old parity. There is no economic or financial significance in the 1925–31 gold standard parity. No doubt, at one time, it possessed some political significance as well as economic justification; the former has given way to the imperative needs of a changed economic situation. When eventually the level of $4·86⅔ was broken through to one several cents lower, the American authorities stated that they attached no importance to the maintenance of an exchange rate having no relevance to the prevailing conditions.

In certain quarters the E.E.A. was severely criticised for its failure to hold the rate at the old parity. Such criticism was based on entirely wrong assumptions regarding the purpose of the E.E.A., the meaning of the Tripartite Currency Agreement and the responsibilities of this country in financial matters to the countries forming the sterling area, not least to itself.

The E.E.A. was never intended to establish or hold sterling at a fixed rate or to oppose rigidly a definite trend disregarding the balance of payments both on income and capital account. Its purpose is to minimise the frequency and extent of fluctuations and to have regard to the continuing necessity to husband its resources for use in future eventualities. There is nothing in the Tripartite Currency Agreement, expressed or implied, which lays upon this country the obligation to maintain a rate of exchange at a fixed level out of alignment with the economic position. On the contrary, liberty of action is reserved to all parties of that agreement in the following clause:

His Majesty's Government must, of course, in its policy towards international monetary relations, take into account the requirements of internal prosperity of the countries of the Empire, as corresponding considerations will be taken into account by the Governments of France and the United States of America.

⟨ 115 ⟩   8-2

As regards the sterling area, which includes the Empire, the advantages accruing from the financial cohesion of all those countries following the lead of Britain would quickly disappear if the guiding principle in exchange rates were determined in Britain not by the economic situation of the whole area but by a shibboleth as represented by a meaningless set of figures called the old parity.

It is the duty of the E.E.A. to intervene in the Exchange and/or Gold Markets to minimise fluctuations. In carrying out that duty it will sometimes gain and at other times lose large amounts of gold, being the counterpart to the ingress and egress of "hot money". Gold is accumulated for the very purpose of releasing it when it is most needed. Such accumulations are built up at varying rates of exchange. It would be unreasonable, therefore, to expect the release of it in unlimited quantities at a fixed level merely for the sake of maintaining a parity having nothing to commend it outside of sentiment or psychology. If that were done the loss of gold would be so great that little if any would remain as a reserve against the possible eventual withdrawal of the huge amounts of foreign capital still remaining here and the liquid capital assets of the sterling area countries. If the gold lost in this manner were counterbalanced by an equal amount of departing refugee capital it would be possible to view such loss with less discomfiture. But that would be asking too much of the forbearance of international speculators. The experience of France in 1936 and 1937 proves conclusively the futility of maintaining a particular rate of exchange when an opinion has been formulated and widely held that that rate cannot be maintained, notwithstanding the large amount of gold used in its defence.

By easing the rate down the E.E.A. has conserved its gold resources and, at the same time, ensured that each successive drop in the exchange value of sterling towards its equilibrium rate with the dollar has added to the forces which, *in toto*, constitute sterling's resistance level.

The foregoing is a brief survey of the causes responsible for the change in ownership of very large quantities of gold. These huge demands or offerings of gold have been concentrated on the E.E.A. It is doubtful if history can provide a precedent of a single agent giving out and taking in the required quantities of gold with such freedom and with so little disturbance to its own domestic background. The range of these transactions successfully carried through by the E.E.A. must be reckoned not in tens of million pounds but in hundreds of millions. That alone is a startling fact. It has, however, a wider significance. It means that fugitive capital has come in and gone out in amounts greater than is indicated by the range of gold holdings of the E.E.A., because there must have been many movements both ways within the highest and lowest limits constituting the range. The term "fugitive capital" is used particularly in its generic sense to include cosmopolitan capital, not excluding British, which is kept in a highly liquid form instantly ready to migrate from the country of temporary habitation to another if a profit or greater security, or both, is offered by so doing. The term also includes foreign capital which at one time has sought safety here, and later, when the reasons for its original flight have disappeared, has returned to the countries of provenance. This kind of money has been named, very aptly, "hot money".

The great changes in the amounts of gold held by the E.E.A. and those held by hoarders, reflecting the views of the latter, and the "flux and reflux of hot money" in this country, have thrown a burden on the Money Market far beyond its capacity to bear without the props plentifully supplied by the E.E.A. Previous chapters have described the methods by which the required assistance by the E.E.A. was achieved at certain critical periods. Up to May 1938 the E.E.A. was called upon to absorb gold in large quantities and to take progressive measures in the Money Market to prevent such absorptions having their normal effect on internal conditions. In the process the borrowing powers were stepped up to a colossal figure. After the French capital withdrawal in May 1938, and during the months following, the E.E.A. has been unwinding itself, shedding its gold very rapidly and piling up large amounts of sterling in Public Deposits. Throughout the Fourth Period, especially in the summer months of 1938, the E.E.A. was severely tested by a crescendo of events ending with the Munich settlement at the end of September. The figures of the E.E.A.'s gold holdings and the figures supplied in Appendix J for this period tell their own tale. They emphasise the volume and range of transactions with which the E.E.A. was called upon to deal in this critical accounting period. They also show that the market and newspaper reports which were current at the time, of the E.E.A.'s gold losses, were exaggerated.

The next chapter is devoted to a review of the E.E.A.'s activities, the problems raised and solved during the time of the September 1938 crisis and its aftermath.

CHAPTER 13

I N the comparatively short period of less than seven years the
E.E.A. has been confronted with many complex problems
and, as we have tried to show in the foregoing chapters, has
overcome them successfully. For the greater part of its short
life the problems which arose were those connected with an
influx of capital and the prevention of such capital having the
otherwise inevitable expansionary effect. Up to 1938 the
problems arising from a reverse flow were minor and infrequent.
The first real test of the E.E.A.'s powers to offset successfully
an efflux of funds from the London Money Market came with
the French capital repatriation in May 1938. There were
difficulties at that time, of course, but they were removed by a
blend of the old remedies, technical innovations, and the
fortuitous aid in the form of the War Loan dividend disbursement. The experience gained during May and June 1938 proved
invaluable for the greater test which reached its climax at the
time of the Munich settlement in the following September. It
is probably correct to state that from the beginning of August
to the end of October the E.E.A. was engaged in the Foreign
Exchange and Money Markets to a greater extent than at any
other time in its history. We think this period of the E.E.A.
working is of such importance as to merit this separate chapter.

The pressure against sterling began about the end of July
when it was realised that the dollar was very much under-
valued. In August the conversion of sterling to dollars gathered
momentum. On a movement which had some economic justi-
fication there was superimposed a demand for dollars, having its
origin in the growing tension in Europe created by the Sudeten
German demands upon the Czecho-Slovakian Government.
The increasing tension leading up to a probability of war compelled many holders of sterling balances in London to convert
such balances to dollars and to a lesser extent Swiss francs,

belgas or florins. Safety of capital was the primary motive behind the enormous transfers which were made during those weeks. Throughout this period the E.E.A. provided the dollars required but only at successively lower levels. A stand was made at certain levels to prevent a runaway movement and in the process large quantities of dollars were sold which were obtained by sales of gold to the American exchange authorities. By operating in support of sterling at different rates the E.E.A. limited the range of fluctuations but it did not rigidly oppose a definite trend, which would have been contrary to its policy. Accordingly the gold holdings of the E.E.A. were utilised in the most effective manner, having regard to the necessity of maintaining a reserve of gold for future eventualities. The climax in the Exchange Market was reached on 28 September 1938, the day before the Munich settlement. In the morning of that day the sterling-dollar exchange rate fell to 4·61, but in the afternoon the rate recovered to 4·72, at which point the E.E.A. bought back, at a profit, large quantities of dollars which it had sold earlier in the day.

The troubles of the E.E.A. did not end with the Munich settlement. The pressure against sterling was resumed because it was believed abroad that Britain would have to embark upon a greatly accelerated programme of rearmament to the detriment of the economic interests of the country. There was also a widespread belief in Europe that the Anglo-American Trade Agreement, when signed, would contain a clause for the realignment of sterling *vis-à-vis* the dollar. As a consequence there were further large demands for dollar exchange and these were satisfied by the E.E.A. but again at successively lower rates of exchange.

The E.E.A. had no difficulty in meeting the requirements of the Exchange Market during the critical months of August, September and October 1938. It certainly had to deal with a volume of business during that time which, probably, was greater than any other three months' period of its history; but the E.E.A. was well able to cope with this large volume. The difficulties experienced were similar to those which developed after the French repatriation in May; the problem presented was that of returning by some means the funds so rapidly withdrawn by the operations in the Exchange Market. In August the replacement of sterling withdrawn by transfers to New York and other places was easily accomplished without much disturbance, but, as the volume of transfers grew, sterling was "bottle-necked" in Public Deposits. So far as the Money Market is concerned, the difference between an efflux of capital and an influx is that in the former sterling is withdrawn from the market *before* its replacement by offsetting operations, and if the movement is prolonged the offsetting operations cannot overtake the withdrawals in time to prevent the development of stringency. During the period under examination the volume of transactions increased with each succeeding day up to the culminating day of 28 September 1938.

In Appendix I we have provided a similar set of figures for the period August–November 1938 as those for the May repatriation. The Bank of England, the tender and tap Treasury Bill figures are given and also the dollar-sterling exchange rates. It will be seen that Public Deposits rose from £9·5 millions on 3 August to £32·2 on 7 September, fell to £11·5 on 28 September, and on 19 October rose to £33·8 millions. The figures for Bankers' Deposits show fluctuations inversely with those for Public Deposits.

Appendix I also shows that Treasury Bill rates were beginning to harden in the first week in September, an indication that the withdrawal of funds unrelieved by offsetting operations and the consequent contractions of the cash basis put the clearing banks in action to restore their depleted cash reserves.

The E.E.A. applied the usual methods of offsetting. Special purchases of Treasury Bills were made in the markets; the gap between national revenue and expenditure was made good out of E.E.A. funds in exchange for tap bills; Treasury Bills offered for tender were reduced and under-allotments of bills were made four times during the period. The amount of net borrowing required to bridge the gap between revenue and expenditure from 6 August to 5 November was £70 millions. Normally most of that money would have been borrowed from the market and tender Treasury Bills would have been increased. Instead, as will be seen in Appendix I, the tender Treasury Bill issue declined over the whole period by £43 millions. Tap bills, on the other hand, increased by £85 millions and the Floating Debt by £47 millions. The recital of these figures proves the valiant efforts made by the E.E.A. to restore the cash position of the market. The fall in tender bills reflects the special buying by the E.E.A. and under-allotments. The rise in tap bills reflects the conversion of tender bills by the E.E.A. to tap bills, and the rise in the Floating Debt is a reflection of the increase in expenditure over national revenue during the period and largely financed by the E.E.A.

But before this measure of restoration of funds to the market was accomplished the E.E.A. was compelled to adopt additional technique to reinforce those normal methods of offsetting mentioned above and in previous chapters. It is possible that the managers of the E.E.A. if they wished could have made a quick restoration of the position by opening deposits with the clearing banks, although the drawback to such a method is that it does not provide direct relief to that section of the market (i.e. banks —other than clearing—discount houses and other financial institutions) which is in need of assistance at such times. The clearing banks relieve any pressure on themselves by calling in short loans from the outside market.

There was, however, another and better method of providing the relief so urgently required, and that was by what is known in the Exchange Market as "swaps". The E.E.A. bought spot dollars, i.e. for delivery in two days, and sold dollars forward, i.e. for delivery one or three months ahead. Although in swaps there are two deals, they are done simultaneously as one transaction and with a margin between the exchange rate fixed for the spot end of the transaction and that for the forward. As forward dollars were quoted at a premium the exchange rate for the spot end was higher than the forward. It must be remembered that the E.E.A. was contemporaneously active in the Exchange Market with two objects in view—to support sterling and conserve its gold holdings. Support for sterling was provided by selling dollars outright for spot delivery, and to the extent that the E.E.A. sold dollars, gold was made available to the American authorities. It is here that the advantages of the swap operations become apparent. The dollars obtained by the spot end of the swap transaction were used in the operations undertaken in support of sterling and thereby avoided the necessity of drawing immediately upon the E.E.A. gold reserves. It is true that when the forward end of the swap transactions matures, the E.E.A. will have to deliver dollars, and unless the contract is renewed, gold must be sold to obtain the dollars.* But in the meantime the trend of dollars may be reversed, in which case replenishment of the dollar or gold holdings of the E.E.A. will be obtained.

The swap transactions were undertaken primarily with the object of returning sterling to the market; and, as these operations were effected with clearing banks *and other banks*, the much-needed sterling funds were distributed over a fairly wide area. Incidentally, as forward dollars were quoted at a premium of about 2 cents the swap operations undertaken by the E.E.A. were equivalent to lending sterling at 1·7 % per annum.

All the above-mentioned measures were effective in restoring the Money Market to normal. But that was not completely accomplished until early in November. The Bank of England statement for 2 November shows that Public and Bankers' Deposits, respectively, were again standing at pre-crisis levels. The monthly figures of clearing-bank averages for this period, which are given on p. 124, also show the restoration of their pre-crisis position except as regards deposits and discounts. These figures need but few comments. In regard to the small decline in deposits in comparison with the market estimates of the total of foreign capital repatriated during this period, it must be pointed out that these figures are clearing-bank figures only. There are no published figures showing the decline in deposits sustained by other banks in this country during the period.

* It is reasonable to assume that the official figure of 21·68 million fine ounces of gold held by the E.E.A. on 30 September 1938 has been arrived at after allowing for the forward dollar sale contracts maturing after that date.

Neither are there any figures available to show the amount of Government securities and other "real" assets sold by foreigners for repatriation of the proceeds. The large increase in acceptances of the clearing banks is a reflection of the swap operations undertaken by the E.E.A. as a means of restoring the cash fund.

1938 (in £ millions)*

	July	August	September	October
Deposits	2308	2298	2268	2256
Cash	244	240	233	234
Call money	158	153	148	148
Discounts	301	304	288	268
Investments	633	641	648	645
Advances	980	970	969	969
Acceptances	115	115	122	129
Cash to deposits	10·6 %	10·5 %	10·3 %	10·4 %

The very large increase in notes circulation during September complicated the position because the Bank of England applied the automatic correction to note withdrawals, that is to say, Government securities were bought; and when, on the passing of the crisis, the notes were returned, securities were sold, notwithstanding the fact that considerable sums were still immobilised in Public Deposits. The automatic corrective applied by the Bank on the return of notes caused some consternation in the Press, but there is no doubt that the Bank is wise to separate its own proper functions from the activities of the E.E.A., however conflicting such a separation may appear to be at times.

There were also complications and contradictory movements in the Gold Market. Throughout August and most of September there were large demands for gold, first by hoarders and later by arbitrageurs who shipped the metal to New York. The E.E.A. freely sold gold for arbitrage to New York as a means of supporting sterling. Then, as the European tension approached a crisis, the war-risk insurance rates were increased prohibitively

* Extracted from the *Financial Times*.

to gold arbitrageurs, whose operations in that direction ceased. When war seemed imminent, hoarded gold was hastily resold because of a fear that if war became actual gold holdings in this country would be sequestered. At this time the E.E.A. bought gold freely, not only to replace its stocks but also to avoid the development of another gold scare.*

There are many useful lessons to be learned by a study of the E.E.A.'s activities during this critical period, and not the least important is that there are limitations to the offsetting principle.

If primary offsetting operations had been completely effective they would have put back into the market with one hand the funds taken out by the other. On completion it might have appeared desirable to put in hand the secondary offsetting operations. If the reverse of the procedure followed at the time of the influx of capital (as in 1936 for instance) were carried out after its exit, we should expect the secondary operation to offset one-tenth part of the withdrawn deposits to take the form of purchases of gold or securities by the E.E.A. from the Bank of England. It is obvious however that the whole series of movements may be short-circuited by combining the primary and secondary offsetting. In the case of an efflux of capital the former expands the credit base by 100% while the latter contracts it by 10%. The aim of the E.E.A. therefore was to replace 90% of the amount repatriated. But the E.E.A. was not able to achieve its aim. The difficulty, as already pointed out, lay in the fact that the sterling required to pay for gold purchases or foreign exchange was withdrawn from the market before it could be replaced, and, as such purchases were continued daily over a long period, the E.E.A. was one step behind and unable to catch up while the pressure against sterling continued.

This phenomenon places limitations upon the doctrine as formerly practised by the E.E.A. and expounded in previous chapters. Therein we observed how an influx of capital under the present regime has precisely the opposite effect to that produced under a gold standard. We are familiar with the definite stringency produced by the influx of capital in 1936—a strin-

* Cf. p. 110.

gency relieved by secondary offsetting operations. In May 1938 the reverse conditions were produced, although secondary offsetting was not undertaken for other unconnected reasons. Up to this point experience has shown that there is a time lag of relatively short duration between the initial major capital movement and the completion of the cycle by primary offsetting operations. In the case of an influx of capital this time lag, regarded as normal, is short, because surplus funds can be drawn off quickly from the market. In the case of an efflux, however, the conditions of the market and the established technique (other than E.E.A.) tend to exaggerate the time lag.

In abnormal circumstances, such as were witnessed from August to October 1938, the inability of the authorities to make their primary operations effective converts the condition usually referred to as the time lag to a state of frustration which persists until the exit of capital is checked or for as long as special alleviating measures fail to overtake the withdrawals. The deflationary effect is very definite during this state of frustration.

This aspect is instructive, because it would seem that in special circumstances such as were experienced before and after the crisis precisely the same conditions are produced under the present monetary regime as were produced after an export of gold under the classical gold standard regime of former times. It is a commonplace that history does sometimes repeat itself. The following is an extract from a letter* written in 1838 by James Pennington, an adviser to the Treasury on financial matters:

If, during the prevalence of an unfavourable foreign exchange the balances (of London bankers with the Bank of England) are reduced by cheques drawn upon the Bank, and finally by payments in gold, for exportation, then—unless the bankers themselves export the gold on their own account which seldom or never happens—the balances due to their various depositors, and consequently the quantity of money in the metropolis, is as effectually reduced as if the outstanding notes of the Bank were reduced by the redemption of securities in its possession, and the bankers' deposits at the Bank of England to remain unaltered.

* Part of a letter quoted in *Studies in the theory of International Trade* by Jacob Viner.

The defect, which proved to be temporary, was largely a question of technique and one which, if one is to judge by the management of the E.E.A. in the past, will be remedied. The value of this aspect of the crisis is the emphasis placed on the need for the E.E.A. to maintain its evolutionary basis.

Probably we are too near the event to make a complete and fair appraisal of all the details which make up the E.E.A.'s handling of the financial machine during the crisis period. But we are not too near to claim that the country owes to it a not inconsiderable debt of gratitude for sparing us the evils and disturbances to which we should have been subject if any other monetary regime had been in force. London during that time was the converging centre of the financial impulses from the whole world and the steadfastness and calm of the London financial machine was largely due to the operations of the E.E.A. and the way in which those operations were carried out.

Whatever may be rightly said about unpreparedness in other aspects of défence, very few can justly accuse the E.E.A. of being unready. The Chancellor of the Exchequer has not been burdened with questions on the working of the E.E.A. during the critical period; but he would have had many put to him if the E.E.A. had not been so well equipped and organised.

CHAPTER 14

THE Exchange Equalisation Account "is an experiment and, as in all experiments, there are possibilities of failure as well as possibilities of success therein".
These words were uttered by the Financial Secretary during a debate in the House of Commons on the setting up of the E.E.A.

The Bank Charter Act 1844 brought to an end the acute controversy concerning the respective merits of the Currency Principle and the Banking Principle. By that enactment former strife in financial matters was resolved by the adoption of a bold experiment. The Currency Principle was enacted, i.e. the note issue without gold backing was limited, notes were made convertible to gold and the bank was compelled to buy all gold offered to it at a fixed price. This was the beginning of the "modern" gold standard, which later was adopted by all the major countries.

Financial history has repeated itself, except in matters of detail, almost a century later. The post-war years, in financial as well as other spheres of life, were notable for the conflict of doctrines. Everywhere there was a turbulent mood which often expressed itself in a desire for the overthrow of many existing institutions, financial and otherwise. In some countries this mood was relieved only by violent methods. In Britain the willingness to compromise and a spirit of tolerance not only prevented militant conflicts but allowed time to be gained for the learning of valuable lessons. The measures adopted were those which the greatest number believed were for the good of the country as a whole. Mistakes were made without a doubt, but they were honest ones, war-weariness being largely responsible. In 1931 we were forced to recognise one of those mistakes.

Unfortunately after six years of increasing distress the world convinced us that we were no longer the chief creditor and that we could neither maintain the gold standard nor buy quite freely from the world, and being humbly minded people and ready to learn we adapted our policy to the changed facts.

Sir Alan Anderson summed up the matter in a letter to the *Statist*, 18 June 1938, from which the above is a quotation.

The adoption of the right policy to the changed financial facts could not have been an easy matter. The suspension of the gold standard was forced upon us whether we wished it or not. A policy in financial matters to follow that act of suspension was a question of urgency. Much depended on the decision. The Empire could have been lost at Jutland in an hour by one man if that man had made a wrong decision at a critical time. The financial policy of the six months which followed the suspension was another Jutland, so far as the Empire was concerned.

The general aim of the Government was to increase production. The essentials for that purpose were—increased tariffs and a managed currency system. Of the latter the guiding principles were (1) to keep the pound sterling free as far as possible from external influences, and (2) the encouragement of cheaper money both for short and long term by every possible technical means. The E.E.A. was designed to carry out the first principle. The technique invented and employed by it was instrumental in achieving the second.

Has the E.E.A. been a success as an "experiment"?

What tests can we apply to enable us to answer that question?

If imitation has anything to commend it as a test, then the answer to our question is simple. The general principle of the British E.E.A. has been copied in most of the major countries of the world, differing only in points of detail to suit local conditions. The aim in all cases has been and is the same. In other countries, such as Scandinavia, where E.E.A.'s have not been set up, the Central Banks of those countries respectively have performed the functions specifically allocated to the E.E.A.'s elsewhere. The technique of the E.E.A.'s, whether carried out by them as such or by Central Banks, has come to be recognised as an essential reinforcing part of a managed currency system.

This line of approach, however, is generalising too much for a fair basis of judgment.

Professor N. F. Hall states that the E.E.A. "was free to fix the prices at which it purchased foreign exchange and gold. Its organisation made it effectively an Account; its policy alone was to determine whether it was to equalise or disturb the exchanges". Writing in 1935, he considered that the E.E.A. had lived up to its name.

The *League of Nations Monetary Review* 1937–38, p. 27, gives the following annual percentage range of variation of sterling in terms of gold and the dollar, since 1934:

	1934	1935	1936	1937
Price of gold (%)	13·1	6·8	4·0	2·4
Rate of dollar (%)	5·7	5·7	4·1	3·2

The *Review* states that "on balance, the price of gold in London declined by 1·5 % during 1937, while the sterling value of the dollar showed a net decline of 1·8 %. Together with sterling all currencies attached to sterling showed, of course, a similar appreciation in terms of the dollar and hence of gold."

If the close range of sterling in terms of gold and dollars may be considered a fair test, the above quotations leave little room for doubt on the point as to whether or not the E.E.A. has fulfilled one of its purposes referred to as "ironing out" fluctuations.

In Appendices L and M there are given the highest and lowest mean daily rates of exchange of the dollar and the franc from 1931 to 1938. The rates given for the franc do not show the same narrow ranges as do those for the dollar. The reason is, of course, that circumstances beyond the control of the British E.E.A. have necessitated a series of declines in the external value of the franc. Nevertheless it is fair to claim that without the active and willing co-operation of the British E.E.A. the extent and frequency of fluctuations in the franc exchange rate would have been very much greater.

In the Empire sterling area exchanges there is no room for fluctuations because the connection with sterling is absolute. The currencies within the group are interchangeable at fixed prices. In the non-Empire sterling area exchanges the connection with sterling is not absolute, but is close enough to limit the margin of fluctuation to a very narrow range.

There is therefore enough evidence to show that where the initiative has been solely with the E.E.A. it has succeeded in reducing the frequency of fluctuations and that in each successive year since inauguration to the end of 1937 it has shortened the range of sterling in terms of the dollar and gold. Where the E.E.A. has not had complete initiative it has contributed to the general good by rendering active assistance whenever possible and within its powers.

From the point of view of the adequacy of the protection the E.E.A. has given to the internal financial and economic structure, it cannot be denied that a great measure of freedom from disturbance through external causes has been vouchsafed. The technique developed and applied by the E.E.A. has followed close upon the heels of all the unfamiliar phenomena which have occurred from time to time.

In the course of its career the E.E.A. and the policy pursued by it have aroused antagonism at home and abroad. In 1933 criticism in France and America, the two main countries of the gold bloc, was particularly bitter on the grounds that the E.E.A. was depressing the pound with the deliberate object of capturing those countries' share of foreign trade. They complained that such a policy had a deflationary effect on world prices, which declined heavily, while the sterling price level was comparatively steady. The answer to that is, the pound was never deliberately depressed below its true economic level; it was sometimes prevented from rising to a level which, if reached, would have given it an over-valuation in terms of other currencies. As regards prices, Britain was, and still is, the largest single buyer of raw materials and commodities, and the countries of supply, in order to retain this market, placed their currencies on a sterling standard. On this point a quotation* from Professor T. E. Gregory may be permitted:

It can be said with confidence that unless the overseas raw material producing areas had followed the downward course of sterling their

* *Memorandum on the possibilities of the Sterling area.*

position would have been positively worsened, since Britain represents to them a major market.... Any single area standing out of the general tendency to peg with sterling would have found itself cut out of the British market, unless it could reduce its internal level of costs sufficiently to adjust the cost of production to the lower level of sterling receipts converted into terms of local currency.

This would seem to reduce the complaints of France and America to one of dissatisfaction with their respective shares of the British market as compared with the proportions they were accustomed to prior to 1931. The responsibility for that situation is not one that can be rightly placed upon the E.E.A.

Commodities at that time were in over-supply; accordingly the prices obtained for those commodities were determined largely by the amount which Britain—the largest buyer—was willing to pay. In a very short while the countries which together formed the sterling area were joined by others. Britain was "piloting a quarter of the world" and a large proportion of the total world trade, so that to reach equilibrium either the sterling price level had to rise considerably to the world or gold price level, or the latter had to decline. For reasons just mentioned sterling prices were dominant and therefore exercised a deflationary pressure on world prices. Again, it was no fault of the E.E.A. if sterling prices did not rise sufficiently to prevent deflationary tendencies developing in the gold countries. The over-abundant supply of commodities did more to depress world prices than the adjustment of sterling to its proper level.

It was the aim of the British Government to raise prices because it recognised that better conditions could not be restored unless the primary producers received more for their commodities than they were then receiving. If the purchasing power of primary producers could be raised by means of higher commodity prices, this country would benefit by their purchases of manufactured goods. In furtherance of that aim the Government took all possible steps. That these were successful may be inferred from the fact that recovery from the depression levels began in the sterling area and later spread to others.

The E.E.A. was criticised on the basis that in 1934 it had

outlived its usefulness and that by its continuance a general return to the gold standard was being hindered. Subsequent events have dissipated the arguments used in support of such criticisms. Stabilisation *may* have been economically justifiable in 1934 but was politically impossible. Then followed the devaluation of the dollar, which may have been economically unjustifiable but was a political necessity.

There were, of course, many criticisms expressed in this country, particularly in the matters of technique. Criticism of this kind was usually based on incomplete knowledge of all the facts, which were known only to the authorities. Viewed over a period, the technique applied by the managers of the E.E.A. has generally been the right one, although to outsiders it may not have appeared to be so at the moment of application.

In matters of policy Professor Charles Rist, writing in the *Revue d'Économie Politique* for 1937, criticises the British E.E.A. on the grounds that it is one of the obstacles to recovery in France and elsewhere. He claims that Britain continues to hoard a large part of the world output of gold for fear that this gold may act on prices in too lively a fashion. He suggests that part of the gold which the E.E.A. acquired should be allowed to fulfil its normal function and expand the credit base. After stating that America very wisely reversed her policy of sterilising gold, he invites Britain "to make a singularly effective contribution to the recovery of international trade" by doing likewise.

One must question the assumption that the E.E.A. has at any time accumulated more gold than is necessary to offset "hot money", a precaution which even Professor Rist considers the E.E.A. is wise in taking. It is questionable also to suggest the similarity of effect by the release of gold in London and New York. There is no basis for such a comparison for the reason that the financial market in London is more highly "geared" than that of New York.

Assuming that the E.E.A. had done in the past what Professor Rist suggests, and allowed part of its gold acquisitions to function naturally, can it be denied that the E.E.A. would have found itself in a position of extraordinary difficulty in the months of July, August and September 1938, when large gold losses occurred? The gold base of the E.E.A. would have been much smaller and in consequence its ability to support the pound in the Gold and Exchange Markets would have been so much less, and the fall in sterling very much greater. Offsetting operations would have been hopelessly compromised.

The Rist and other plans must be judged on the ground of their ability to assist the present machinery of monetary control, the key point of which is the E.E.A. Here it would be an advantage to state the main reasons for the success of the E.E.A. apart from the essential background provided by balanced budgets and a system of national finance which the world regards as correct. Firstly, the E.E.A. *borrows* the funds it needs to function; secondly, against its collateral of Treasury Bills it acquires gold; thirdly, by the application of the principle of offsetting, the final relationship in these transactions is—the E.E.A. is the borrower, and the foreigner the lender. Any experimental scheme which radically departs from the common ideas of sound finance would expose this country again to the humbling experiences of 1929–31. The flow of funds would be immediately reversed. Under these conditions the E.E.A. would not be in a position to borrow without producing deflation; it could not acquire gold because the flow of funds would be the other way, and it would be unable to offset the effect of its own borrowings.

Such plans have this in common. They increase the credit base without ensuring the demand for the additional credit. If that is so the only result is to create "bottle-necks" of cash in the banks or in the long-term capital market which, for lack of other outlets, would be utilised in the only possible way—in Treasury Bills. That is to say, if any of these plans had been in operation at the time of the large gold drain during the period mentioned above when sterling was piled up in Public Deposits, both the banks and the E.E.A. would have competed for the limited supply of bills; truly a ridiculous spectacle.

The Rist de-sterilisation plan requires the complete abandonment of those principles of the E.E.A. which have proved so efficacious in the past.

It would seem to be preferable to retain an organisation which in the past five years has not only warded off many financial perils but has brought to the country great benefits, not least the loan of vast sums of foreign money without security at the lowest possible rate of interest. The existence of that foreign money in London was instrumental in bringing down the short- and long-term interest rate which paved the way for the great conversion schemes and gave industries in this country the inestimable benefits of cheap money. The E.E.A. is essential if we are to avoid the old evils which the Bank of England with its own limited resources is unable to offset by open-market operations.

The suggestion that the E.E.A. hoards more gold than it need to give the financial system complete freedom from the rest-lessness of cosmopolitan capital does not appear to be supported by facts. The *League of Nations Monetary Review* 1937–38 on p. 23 gives the central foreign assets reserves of fifteen "sterling group" countries as at the end of each year from 1931 to 1937. During this period the balances increased from £79·6 to £252·3 millions. The *Review* points out that "as these countries keep their exchanges in a fixed relationship with sterling, it is reason-able to assume that the bulk of their foreign balances are held in London; they appear to be largely invested in Treasury Bills through the Bank of England. To the extent that these balances are acquired in transactions with countries outside the sterling area, their transfer to London tends to be neutralised by the Exchange Equalisation Fund in the same way as the inflow of refugee capital. To the extent however that they are acquired in transactions with the United Kingdom itself, their investment in Treasury Bills is not accompanied by an increase in the supply of bills on account of the Exchange Equalisation Fund, and therefore tends to reduce money rates in London."

To the figure of £252·3 millions, being the Central Bank reserves of fifteen sterling area countries, there must be added an unascertainable but very large amount of sterling held by the commercial banks and industrial companies domiciled in those countries. In addition there are large sums held here by Central Banks, commercial banks and industrial companies of foreign countries which are not included in the sterling area. Such money is sent here because it can be more remuneratively employed, or for reasons of safety. Finally, there is that large bulk of foreign capital described as "hot money".

The outsider is not in a position to give the exact figures applicable to each group mentioned above. The tabulation of such figures is made by the Bank of England from statements rendered to it by all banks operating in London, following a recommendation on these lines by the Macmillan Committee, but the Bank very wisely does not make public the results of the tabulation. We do know, however, that the total of sterling held here for non-domestic account must be very large.* From the point of view of the E.E.A. it matters not whether such sterling was acquired in transactions with the United Kingdom or otherwise. What is of importance to it is this: the countries which own sterling held here are operating a system which closely resembles a gold exchange standard because they can at any time utilise the sterling they possess in the purchase of gold. The gold they acquire must come from the British E.E.A. and the amount not converted is a potential demand for gold at some future time.

Allowing some deduction from the total of sterling assets held here to represent that part which in any circumstances would remain here, there is left a very large sum against which the E.E.A. should hold gold if it is to be in a position to fulfil all possible demands. If we consider that the gold held by the Bank of England is no more than sufficient for internal needs plus a margin for emergencies, there is left the amount held by the E.E.A., which at March 1938 was £298 millions, to meet the possible withdrawal of £252 millions of Central Bank assets, plus the large unascertainable amounts representing the sterling assets of the other groups mentioned above.

Clearly the E.E.A. does not hold more gold than it may be called upon to deliver at a moment's notice. On the contrary,

* In the second half of 1938 considerable sums were repatriated.

it may well be asked if the E.E.A. has sufficient gold to meet these demands.* It must be remembered that since March 1938 the E.E.A. has lost large sums by the French repatriation and in support of sterling from the causes described in the previous chapter. To the extent that such gold losses were counterbalanced by the departure of an equal amount of "hot money", well and good, but the amount not so counterbalanced is a loss on capital account and a definite weakening of the E.E.A. so far as its gold assets are affected.

Reverting to the history of the E.E.A. it is to its credit that the organisation and management facilitated a better distribution of gold by the implied, though uncovenanted, right of all those countries having sterling balances to convert them to gold if they wished to do so, whether the yearly increment was earned by them in this country or not. That many have done so is shown by the gold export figures of this country and the increased holdings in weight and value of many Central Banks. Where else but London is it possible to obtain gold merely by the previous acquisition of the respective currency?

The advantages accruing to foreign countries by the holding of sterling are being more widely appreciated. The Daladier franc was given a maximum depreciation in terms of sterling, no mention being made of the dollar or other currencies.† At the end of August Holland and Switzerland allowed their currencies to be tied to sterling when the pressure against the latter was strong. In effect, these three countries placed themselves at that time on the fringe of the sterling "club". That may be flattering but it can also be dangerous from this country's point of view, for this reason. By placing their currencies in alignment with sterling, France, Holland and Switzerland have converted the original pressure against sterling to an appreciation of the dollar in terms of those four European currencies. Holland, for instance, in severing the link with the dollar, allowed the florin to depreciate in terms of that currency. To bring that about the

* Since the above was written the gold holdings of the E.E.A. have been considerably augmented. See Addenda, p. 143.

† In November 1938 M. Reynaud announced that the franc would remain "faithful to sterling".

Dutch authorities most probably sold florins and bought dollars, and they must continue to do so if they wish to maintain the sterling peg. If the American authorities make gold available to the Dutch in exchange for dollars then an encroachment on British gold does not take place. On the other hand if gold from America is not so obtained, dollars will be sold by the Dutch authorities for sterling, with which gold can be obtained in the London market. In this case there is an encroachment on the gold holdings of the E.E.A.; that is to say, gold accumulated in the past as counterpart to refugee money entering this country would have to be released for reasons quite unconnected with that refugee capital which may still be held here. There are indications that such tactics have been pursued, and it is a dangerous development.

This situation is aggravated by the existence of a trade balance in favour of Holland and Switzerland and against Britain, as the net balance may be used to obtain gold. This feature, of course, applies to all the countries of the sterling area having a favourable trade balance with Britain. They are entitled to remove the surplus in gold if they wish. At the same time the equivalent of their respective adverse balances with America should be left in this country, as otherwise the whole brunt of an adverse balance, not only of Britain but of all those countries in the sterling area and those on the fringe of it, would fall upon this country in the form of gold losses by the E.E.A. The encroachment on the British E.E.A. gold holdings need not take place if all countries maintaining a gold-exchange sterling standard make gold available to Britain out of their own supplies, the amount representing their individual net balance of payments due to America less the net balance of payments due from Britain.

The foregoing are some of the problems with which the managers of the E.E.A. are confronted. There are many of a short-term character calling for radical and speedy treatment as they arise, and there are others not immediately apparent but none the less insidious. Very often, too, the aims of the E.E.A. conflict. If the E.E.A. is too successful in achieving its aim of "ironing out" fluctuations it may thus cover up important economic trends which, if allowed to operate naturally, would express themselves either in a change in the level of the currency in terms of other currencies, or in an expansion or contraction, as the case may be, in the internal cost structure. The masking of economical trends may have deleterious effects. In fact such a result has already been produced. The holding of sterling in 1937–38 at a level which under-valued the dollar manifested itself in a considerable deterioration of the balance of payments of this country as expressed in the large excess of imports, even after making due allowance for rearmament requirements.

Let us suppose that during this period Britain and America had operated a full gold standard. As the adverse balance of payments developed sterling would have come under pressure and the exchange rate would have approached the gold-export point. If the adverse balance continued, gold would have been taken from the Bank of England and shipped to America. The loss of gold in this country would have contracted the credit base and the gain of gold would have expanded credit in America. This self-regulatory process, if left unhindered, would have adjusted the price levels in the two countries, and equilibrium would have been reached.

Under the present system and the Tripartite Currency Agreement there is no automatic correction. For the latter part of 1937 and the first half of 1938 American export prices were 10% below the British, and although gold in large quantities has been shipped to America there has been no contraction here or expansion on the credit base in America as a result of this movement of gold.* An expansionary condition has been produced in America from totally different causes, such as deliberate monetary action. It is possible that this inflationary spending may produce a rise in American prices, in which case some part of the under-valuation of the dollar will be corrected. But until that happens Britain's adverse balance of payments must give cause for concern in the absence of some corrective which,

* In April 1938 the Inactive Gold Fund ($1183 millions) in America was monetised. After that date all gold arrivals in excess of a quarterly inflow of $100 millions are similarly monetised.

under a managed currency system, should take the form of exchange adjustment.*

It is no part of our duty to suggest what America should do. This country's interests would be served without doing damage to America's legitimate interests if the Tripartite Currency Agreement is applied in accordance with its spirit as well as the expressed intentions. The great advantage of that Agreement is that it gives a workable basis to the E.E.A. That feature is worth some sacrifice for its retention. Nevertheless, the disadvantage of the Agreement is this: the application of it has placed undue emphasis upon the elimination of fluctuations in the exchange rate, notwithstanding the appearance of danger signals indicating that the exchange level maintained is not a correct one.

Professor N. F. Hall, writing in 1935, asserted that

In the short period, for the maintenance of continuity in financial and commercial transactions, it is clearly desirable that the limits of variations in market quotations should be the criterion observed by the managing authority. But for the maintenance of economic inter-relationships of a more fundamental character, wider variations in market fluctuations may be appropriate.

Events in 1937–38 concerning the E.E.A. have underlined the truth of that assertion.

The conflict between short-term and long-term aims is responsible for such dilemmas confronting the E.E.A. as were described in the previous chapter; therein it was shown that the support given to sterling delayed the realisation of an exchange rate which, if accomplished, would have ended the pressure against sterling.

Reviewing the achievements of the E.E.A. it can be said, without partiality, that the managing authorities deserve the gratitude of the country they serve. Each problem has been dealt with as it arose, not by reference to hard and fast rules which may or may not have been laid down, but by clever

* At the end of 1938, the dollar-sterling exchange rate was $4·64½. Thus, the greater part of the former over-valuation of sterling has been adjusted.

adaptations of existing technique or the designing of new. Where established technique or tradition has stood in the way of a solution it has been swept aside to permit the trial of new methods. In most cases they have succeeded. The E.E.A. commenced life as an audacious experiment, bitterly criticised in its early days because it was not comprehended. To-day it is regarded everywhere as the essential linch-pin of our monetary equipment. It has steadfastly pursued the three main principles governing operations and has faithfully carried out the intentions of Parliament.

The E.E.A. can no longer be regarded as a stop-gap pending the establishment of a new form of gold standard. The prerequisite conditions for that event are nowhere apparent. All that has happened in recent years, especially in 1938, has stressed the importance of retaining for the time being some freedom in such vital matters as the external value of the pound or its corollary, the internal purchasing power of the currency. When, eventually, this country returns to some form of gold standard there is little doubt that the main principles of the E.E.A. will be incorporated in it, though of course its *raison d'être* will have changed. Whether, as Professor Hall strongly urges, the E.E.A. will be amalgamated with the Issue Department of the Bank of England, or not, depends on future events.

Monetary historians of the future will note the devastated areas in the nineteen-twenties and thirties, scourged by the financial "locusts"; but they may also note that from 1932 onwards, although the "locusts" multiplied and continued to travel on the prevailing wind, when they alighted they were corralled into smoke-encircled places where they could do no harm. That may be considered by future historians as a very great achievement. London invented the Exchange Equalisation Account which applied the remedy for these disturbances and did not bother about the patent rights.

It is fitting to conclude this book with a quotation from a speech* by Sir John Simon, the Chancellor of the Exchequer,

* Official Report, *Parliamentary Debates*, vol. 343, no. 41, 1175.

on 9 February 1939, on the third reading of the Currency
and Bank Notes Bill 1939.*

He said:

"...the Exchange Equalisation Account is one of our great sources
of strength. We were the first country to show the world how to do
it. It is being done with great skill, and we owe a great deal to the
devoted men, whose work is never published, who watch this matter
and serve the country so well in trying to maintain our currency
value."

* See Addenda, p. 143.

ADDENDA

This book was already in the press when three Treasury and/or Bank of England announcements were made in rapid succession. Alterations to the text to conform to the changes and effects of these announcements were not possible. Accordingly, they are dealt with in these "Addenda".

The first announcement was made on 5 January 1939 when the Chancellor of the Exchequer made known to the market through the Bank of England his wish that the banks bring to bear the closest scrutiny on foreign exchange and gold operations with the view to the elimination of all transactions of a speculative nature.

It was considered that the facilities of the London Exchange and Money Markets were being abused by international speculators who were engaged upon attacks against the pound. It was not intended, however, to interfere in any way with the legitimate transactions, either in the Gold or Exchange Markets, of commercial interests.

It is understood that the authorities in America, France and Holland co-operated with the British in suppressing activities of the cosmopolitan speculator whose only concern is profit.

Early in January 1939 the dollar-sterling exchange rate did not show the expected signs of recovery from the low levels reached in December 1938. Many forward exchange contracts falling due in January were renewed for further periods and in consequence the support for sterling which would have been afforded by the closing of such contracts was not forthcoming. Similarly, forward operations in gold were extended and, in many cases, financed on borrowed money. The effect of the Treasury request will be the closing of many exchange and gold contracts.

The second announcement was more spectacular. On 6 January 1939 the Bank of England announced the transfer of

£200,001,571 of bar gold from the Issue Department to the E.E.A. in exchange, presumably, for tap bills. At the same time it was stated that Parliamentary authority would be sought to amend the Currency and Bank Notes Act 1928 to permit an increase in the upper limit of the Fiduciary Issue from £260 to £400 millions.

In Chapter 9, p. 86, attention was drawn to the transfer of gold from the E.E.A. to the Bank of England against a reduction in the Fiduciary Issue from £260 to £200 millions. It was suggested that, by this action, the authorities may have intended to impart some elasticity to this item in the control of the money fabric and it was indicated that, at some future time, the Fiduciary Issue might be increased if the state of the E.E.A.'s gold assets warranted a transfer of gold to it from the Bank of England.

It was generally expected, however, that if such a transfer ever became necessary it would be limited to the extent of the difference between the Fiduciary Issue, as it then stood, and the figure of £260 millions—the statutory limit. By transferring the huge mass of £200 millions (£353 millions at market price) as an addition to the not inconsiderable holding of the E.E.A. and increasing the assets of the Fiduciary Issue to an amount which would permit such transfer, the whole world was made aware of the authorities' intention to support sterling at a level they desired, and was given impressive evidence of the means available to give effect to such intention.

The magnitude of the operation was a masterstroke which placed the E.E.A. in an impregnable position.

The third announcement was even more spectacular and unexpected.

On 1 February 1939 the following statement was issued:

The Chancellor of the Exchequer to-day presented a Bill to deal with the fiduciary note issue of the Bank of England, which was foreshadowed at the time of the recent transfer of gold from the Bank of England to the Exchange Equalisation Account.

Under the Bill the gold and other assets of the Issue Department will in future be valued weekly at current prices. Any excess of their total value over the total note issue will be transferred to the Exchange Equalisation Account and conversely the latter Account will make good any deficiency.

At present the gold in the Issue Department is valued at the old price of 85*s.* an ounce: under the Bill it will be written up to its current market value, and as the gold will remain in the Issue Department it will be possible to fix the fiduciary note issue at £300,000,000 instead of its present temporary figure of £400,000,000.

The Bill referred to in the above statement is called "The Currency and Bank Notes Act 1939". It passed into law on 28 February 1939. The text of the Act is given on p. 152.

The main point is the intention to write-up the gold stocks in the Issue Department of the Bank of England, which, after the above-mentioned transfer was made, amounted to £126,414,357 (29,760,520 fine ounces at the old statutory price). At a market price of 148*s.* 5*d.* per fine ounce the monetary value of this holding is increased to £220,847,857. Since 6 January 1939 the total of securities forming the backing to the Fiduciary Note Issue stood at the figure of £400 millions, in accordance with the announcement of 6 January and referred to in the above addendum. The revaluation of the gold stocks increases the assets to a total of £620 millions which would permit a huge and unwanted increase in the note issue. It is proposed, therefore, to reduce the Fiduciary Issue from £400 to £300 millions, by transferring £100 millions in securities to the E.E.A.

The revaluation of the gold at current market price will produce an unrealised capital appreciation of about £95 millions which falls short of the reduction in the Fiduciary Issue by £5 millions. We shall return to this point later. Any future profits of the Issue Department will accrue to the E.E.A. and not, as formerly, to the Treasury.

The gold and other assets of the Issue Department are to be subject to a weekly valuation at current market prices. Any excess of such valuation over the total note issue will be transferred *to* the E.E.A.; any deficiency will be made good *by* the E.E.A.

The Chancellor of the Exchequer stated at the second reading of the Bill that on the first valuation there will be made good to the Issue Department a sum of £9 millions, being the approximate amount by which the total securities forming the backing to the Fiduciary Issue is deficient as compared with the market valuation of those securities. This deficiency will be made good by the E.E.A. Thereafter any differences will be settled to or from the E.E.A. and such differences may be made in securities, gold or cash, whichever is appropriate. It is obvious, however, that securities can be used for settlements only when they are required to bring the assets of the Fiduciary Issue up to market valuation. Transfers to make good deficiencies in the valuation of gold assets can only be gold or cash.

If the Fiduciary Issue backing is full in the sense that all the securities correspond to market prices, a transfer of securities from the E.E.A. to make good a short-fall in the valuation of the gold assets would affect the Banking Department, where the item "Government Securities" would rise and "Notes" would fall. This procedure, of course, would weaken the reserve and does not appear to be the intentions of the Bill, which authorises a transfer of assets from the E.E.A. to the Issue Department only.

The writing-down of the Fiduciary Issue from £400 to £300 millions and the writing-up of the gold holding from £126 to £221 millions will produce a figure of £521 millions as the total of the assets in the Issue Department. As the total of notes issued amounted to £526 millions (approximately) on 1 February 1939, there will have to be made an adjustment of about £5 millions to equalise these totals. Either the notes in issue must be reduced by £5 millions by drawing on the Banking Department reserve, or gold for the amount must be transferred from the E.E.A. to the Issue Department and so bring the total of assets up to the total of notes issued, viz. £526 millions. The former alternative is unlikely, for reasons explained above. The method adopted to adjust this difference will be apparent on the first weekly statement issued after the Royal Assent has been given to the Currency and Bank Notes Act 1939.*

* On 1 March 1939 gold to the value of £5,566,983 was transferred from the E.E.A. to the Issue Department to equalise the total assets with total liabilities then outstanding.

When these adjustments have been made, the E.E.A. will have gained £91 millions in securities and lost over £5 millions in gold. The net gain of £86 millions is an addition to the total resources of the E.E.A. and is to be merged with its other assets. The potential fund of the E.E.A. will be in the region of £706 millions.*

At the beginning of August and at Christmas each year, when an increase in the note circulation for temporary periods is normal, such increases may be ensured either by a temporary enlargement of the Fiduciary Issue in accordance with the terms of the Currency and Bank Notes Act 1928 (which is not repealed), or by a transfer of gold from the E.E.A. to the Issue Department. A transfer of securities for this purpose would not suffice, for the above-mentioned reasons.

At other times when an increase in notes in circulation comes about through a quickening of industrial and commercial life, the additional notes required will be supplied out of the reserve of the Bank of England. When the reserve falls to a level regarded as imprudent and further notes are required, it may be reinforced by the E.E.A. through the Issue Department by means of a transfer of gold in the manner described in Chapter 7. On p. 59 it was pointed out that, in this matter of gold purchases by the Issue Department, the difference between the procedure under the present monetary system and that under a gold standard is that under the latter gold governs the amount of notes, while under the former the note issue governs the amount of gold held in the Issue Department. We said that the brunt of this reversed order of procedure falls upon the reserve of the Bank of England. The new Bill gives legislative effect to this reversal, but after enactment the brunt will not necessarily fall upon the reserve but upon the E.E.A. This, therefore, is a new function of the E.E.A. In the past it has been called upon to equalise the exchanges and credit; in future it will have the added duty of equalising the currency of the country. The appropriate title now is "The Exchange and Currency Equalisation Account".

* See table on p. 150.

One hundred years ago the Banking school urged an unlimited note issue so long as notes were convertible; the Currency school, on the other hand, wanted the banks to be obliged to reduce notes in proportion to the gold exported.

The Bank Charter Act 1844 rejected the former principle and compromised on the latter. The Currency and Bank Notes Act 1939 carries this compromise to a point rendered necessary by modern developments and removes an anachronism which serves little more purpose than a link with the 1844 Act. Section 4 of that Act, which compels the Bank to give notes in exchange for gold bullion at 77s. 9d. per standard ounce, is to be repealed. If it is true, as Andreades has claimed, that "all systems risk one or other of two dangers: either the paper currency is unduly restricted or it is left so free as to endanger its security",* then it seems that we have evolved over a period of years a happy compromise, expressed in legal form in the new Act.

Whether we have achieved the ideal managed currency system—conscious, skilful control in place of the ruthless automaticity of the gold standard—only the future will show.

When setting up the E.E.A., Parliament in its wisdom did not lay down hard and fast rules under which the E.E.A. would operate. It contented itself with the provision of the necessary funds, permitted secrecy to surround the operations of the E.E.A., and designated the method of winding-up and disposal of its assets. This aspect of empiricism in our national affairs has been a particularly happy one in regard to the E.E.A. The organisation, principles and technique have been quietly and efficiently developed—experience being the guide and mentor—and, over a period of years, skilful minds have been at work evolving a system that will respond to all the manifold needs of this country without inflicting damage on any part of it.

In retrospect it is difficult to avoid the conviction that the authorities decided long ago on the idea which has taken shape in the Currency and Bank Notes Act 1939, and that they have

* *History of the Bank of England,* by A. Andreades, Vol. II, Chapter IV, p. 277.

waited for what they regard as a suitable opportunity to make public their intentions.

It is true that the primary purpose of the Bill is to bring the Issue Department's assets, as recorded in the weekly statement, into an accord with the market realities. It is a matter of book-keeping machinery. Valuable as this objective realism is, it is probable that historians will honour the Act as the legislative birth of a new financial system which, as *The Times* suggests, may come to be known as the "market value gold standard".

In view of the importance of the large gold transfer referred to above and the new Bill, we think it may be useful to show on the following page the effect of these items on the E.E.A., and this has been done by adjusting the table facing p. 82 to the new conditions.

As explained on p. 83, item (*a*) will remain immobilised until the E.E.A. is wound up. Item (*b*) is the book profit which will accrue to the E.E.A. only if this portion of its gold stock is realised in such a manner as will produce the equivalent of the market price, and item (*c*) is the amount available for further purchases of gold, if prior sales have not been made. There is, of course, an additional but unknown amount available for gold purchases, representing the jobbing profits made on exchange and gold operations since commencement.

The "fixed value" used in the past for transactions between the E.E.A. and the Bank, as explained on p. 83, will no longer apply after enactment of the new Bill. The basis of such transfers, in future, is to be the market valuation,* a simplification in accounting that is desirable and welcome.

In all other respects—policy, operation and technique—the E.E.A. will remain the same and as described in previous pages of this book. The sterling exchange rate, the market price of gold and the basis of credit have not been stabilised by the new proposals. The authorities are free to allow changes in all three spheres if, in their judgment, the prevailing conditions warrant

* On the first valuation, 1 March 1939, a price of 148*s*. 5*d*. per fine ounce was used for purposes of valuation of gold assets.

ATTEMPTED RECONSTRUCTION OF OFFICIAL AND OTHER FIGURES OF THE EXCHANGE EQUALISATION ACCOUNT

30 *September* 1938

(Fourth Accounting Period)

Plus the transfer of £200,001,571 of bar gold from the Bank of England on 6 January 1939, and transfer of assets from Issue Department as required by the Currency and Bank Notes Act 1939.

(In £ millions)

	Assets	Liabilities
Total loans from Consolidated Fund ...		550·00
Balance of old Dollar Exchange Account		25·00
Loss on dollar and franc credits ...	8·00	
Net gold purchases to March 1938 =291·15		
Net gold sales April to Sept. 1938 =147·07		
Cost of net gold holding 30 Sept. 1938 ...	144·08	
(21,684,000 fine oz.)		
Cost of gold transferred from Bank of England, 6 Jan. 1939	200·00	
(47,084,375 fine oz. at 84s. 11½d. per oz.)		

Difference on:
Book loss on gold transferred to Bank of England, Sept. 1931 to Sept. 1937. See Table facing p. 82. (Immobilised asset) ...   . $110·73(a)$
Book profit on 47,084,375 fine oz. (£200,001,571) transferred 6 Jan. 1939 *from* Bank of England, less 750,183 fine oz. (£5,566,983) approx. transferred *to* Bank of England on 1 March 1939 in accordance with Currency and Bank Notes Act 1939 = 46,334,192 fine oz. at 84s. 11½d. = £196,814,674
46,334,192 fine oz. at say 150s. = £347,506,440 $150·69(b)$

... with brace ... **39·96**

Securities transferred 1 March 1939 from the Issue Department against a reduction in the Fiduciary Issue, in accordance with the Currency and Bank Notes Act 1939, less £9 millions, being deficiency in valuation of non-gold assets		91·00
Amount of resources utilised	352·08	
Amount of liquid resources apparently available	$203·19(c)$	
Amount of prospective liquid resources...	$150·69(b)$	
	705·96	705·96

Proportion of loss on dollar and franc credits to total fund (as augmented) ...   .   1·13 %
Proportion of gold, at cost, to total fund ...   ...   48·74 %
Proportion of liquid resources apparently available to total fund (c) ...   .   28·78 %
Proportion of prospective liquid resources to total fund (b) 21·35 %

100·00 %

such changes. The managers of the E.E.A. in future will have the choice of a variety of statutes which will give them an elasticity of technique for application when necessary in any foreseeable circumstance. As shown in the percentage table on page 150, the assets available are sufficiently large and diverse to give and ensure to the managers a paramount influence in the Foreign Exchange, Gold, Money and Stock Markets.

The writer of the Foreword to this book has very succinctly summed up the post-war history in monetary affairs in the following words to the author:

In the years 1925–1931 we tried to operate a gold standard which the world used as a sterling-exchange standard. Since 1931 we have tried to operate a sterling-exchange standard which the world increasingly uses as a gold standard. We seem, at last, to have found a system that works without detriment to ourselves.

An Act to amend the law with respect to the Issue
Department of the Bank of England, the Exchange
Equalisation Account and the issue and place of pay-
ment of Bank of England notes [28 February 1939].

BE it enacted by the King's most Excellent Majesty, by
and with the advice and consent of the Lords Spiritual and
Temporal, and Commons, in this present Parliament
assembled, and by the authority of the same, as follows:

Amount of
fiduciary
note issue
18 & 19
Geo. 5,
c. 13

1. The fiduciary note issue shall, unless and until, after
the commencement of this Act, it is reduced under subsection (2) of section two of the Currency and Bank Notes
Act, 1928, or increased under subsection (1) of section eight
of that Act, be three hundred million pounds and accordingly—

  (*a*) in subsection (1) of the said section two and sub-
    section (1) of the said section eight, for the words
    "two hundred and sixty million pounds" there shall
    be substituted the words "three hundred million
    pounds"; and

  (*b*) any Treasury Minute in force at the commencement
    of this Act under the said section eight shall cease to
    have effect.

Valua-
tions of
assets of
Issue
Depart-
ment

2. (1) The assets held in the Issue Department of the
Bank of England (in this Act referred to as "the Department") shall be valued on the day on which this Act comes
into operation and thereafter once in each week.

(2) For the purposes of every such valuation, the assets
shall be valued at such prices as may be certified by the
Bank of England to be the current prices of those assets
respectively on the day of the valuation, ascertained in such
manner as may be agreed between the Treasury and the
Bank:

Provided that adjustments may, if the Treasury so
direct, be made in respect of interest affecting the current
price of any securities and, in the case of securities standing
at a premium, in respect of that premium.

⟨ 152 ⟩

(3) If, as the result of any such valuation, the value of the assets then held in the Department differs from the total amount of the Bank of England notes then outstanding, there shall be paid to the Department from the Exchange Equalisation Account (in this Act referred to as "the Account") or to the Account from the Department such sum as will counteract that difference, and separate payments may be made in respect of differences arising from changes in the value of gold and differences arising from changes in the value of other assets.

Any payment required by this subsection may be effected in cash or, by agreement between the Treasury and the Bank of England, by a transfer of gold or securities (whichever is appropriate), or partly in cash and partly by such a transfer.

3. (1) Gold held in the Department may be sold to the Account and gold may be bought for the Department from the Account, in each case at the price at which gold was valued for the purposes of the last valuation under the last preceding section. *Consequential provisions*

(2) The Treasury shall pay into the Account all sums received by them after the commencement of this Act in respect of the profits of the Department under section six of the Currency and Bank Notes Act, 1928.

4. (1) Notwithstanding anything in any enactment, bank notes for five pounds and upwards may be issued by the Bank of England otherwise than at their head office without being made payable at the place of issue, and all bank notes for five pounds and upwards issued by the Bank shall, wherever issued, be payable only at the head office of the Bank unless expressly made payable also at some other place. *Miscellaneous provisions as to Bank of England notes*

(2) Section four of the Bank Charter Act, 1844 (which requires the Department to issue notes in return for gold), shall cease to have effect. *7 & 8 Vict. c. 32*

5. (1) This Act may be cited as the Currency and Bank Notes Act, 1939. *Short title,*

(2) This Act shall come into operation on the first Wednesday after the day on which the Royal Assent is given thereto. *commencement and repeal*

(3) The enactments set out in the Schedule to this Act are hereby repealed to the extent mentioned in the third column of that Schedule.

SCHEDULE

Section 5.   ENACTMENTS REPEALED

Session and Chapter	Short Title	Extent of Repeal
7 Geo. 4, c. 46	The Country Bankers Act, 1826	The final proviso to section fifteen
3 & 4 Will. 4, c. 98	The Bank of England Act, 1833	Section four
7 & 8 Vict. c. 32	The Bank Charter Act, 1844	Section four
22 & 23 Geo. 5, c. 25	The Finance Act, 1932	Subsections (2) to (6) of section twenty-five

APPENDIX A

GOLD STANDARD ACT 1925

An Act to facilitate the return to a gold standard and for purposes connected therewith. (13 May 1925.)

BE it enacted by the King's most Excellent Majesty, by and with the advice and consent of the Lords Spiritual and Temporal, and Commons, in this present Parliament assembled, and by the authority of the same, as follows:

1. (1) Unless and until His Majesty by Proclamation otherwise directs: *Issue of gold coin suspended and right to purchase gold bullion*

   (a) The Bank of England, notwithstanding anything in any Act, shall not be bound to pay any note of the Bank (in this Act referred to as "a bank note") in legal coin within the meaning of section six of the Bank of England Act, 1833, and bank notes shall not cease to be legal tender by reason that the Bank do not continue to pay bank notes in such legal coin:

   (b) Subsection (3) of section one of the Currency and Bank Notes Act, 1914 (which provides that the holder of a currency note shall be entitled to obtain payment for the note at its face value in gold coin) shall cease to have effect:

   (c) Section eight of the Coinage Act, 1870 (which entitles any person bringing gold bullion to the Mint to have it assayed, coined and delivered to him) shall, except as respects gold bullion brought to the Mint by the Bank of England, cease to have effect.

   (2) So long as the preceding subsection remains in force, the Bank of England shall be bound to sell to any person who makes a demand in that behalf at the head office of the Bank during the office hours of the Bank, and pays the purchase price in any legal tender, gold bullion at the price of three pounds, seventeen shillings and tenpence halfpenny per ounce

⟨ 155 ⟩

troy of gold of the standard of fineness prescribed for gold coin by the Coinage Act, 1870, but only in the form of bars containing approximately four hundred ounces troy of fine gold.

Power for Treasury to borrow for exchange operations

2. (1) Any money required for the purpose of exchange operations in connection with the return to a gold standard may be raised within two years after the passing of this Act in such manner as the Treasury think fit, and for that purpose they may create and issue, either within or without the United Kingdom and either in British or in any other currency, such securities bearing such rate of interest and subject to such conditions as to repayment, redemption or otherwise as they think fit, and may guarantee in such manner and on such terms and conditions as they think proper the payment of interest and principal of any loan which may be raised for such purpose as aforesaid:

Provided that any securities created or issued under this section shall be redeemed within two years of the date of their issue, and no guarantee shall be given under this section so as to be in force after two years from the date upon which it is given.

(2) The principal and interest of any money raised under this Act, and any sums payable by the Treasury in fulfilling any guarantee given under this Act, together with any expenses incurred by the Treasury in connection with, or with a view to the exercise of, their powers under this section shall be charged on the Consolidated Fund of the United Kingdom or the growing produce thereof.

(3) Where by an Appropriation Act passed after the commencement of this Act power is conferred on the Treasury to borrow money up to a specified amount, any sums which may at the time of the passing of that Act have been borrowed or guaranteed by the Treasury in pursuance of this section and are then outstanding shall be treated as having been raised in exercise of the power conferred by the said Appropriation Act and the amount which may be borrowed under that Act shall be reduced accordingly.

Short title

3. This Act may be cited as the Gold Standard Act, 1925.

APPENDIX B

CURRENCY AND BANK NOTES ACT 1928

An Act to amend the law relating to the issue of bank notes by the Bank of England and by banks in Scotland and Northern Ireland, and to provide for the transfer to the Bank of England of the currency notes issue and of the assets appropriated for the redemption thereof, and to make certain provisions with respect to gold reserves and otherwise in connection with the matters aforesaid and to prevent the defacement of bank notes. (2 July 1928.)

BE it enacted by the King's most Excellent Majesty, by and with the advice and consent of the Lords Spiritual and Temporal, and Commons, in this present Parliament assembled, and by the authority of the same, as follows:

1. (1) Notwithstanding anything in any Act—

   (a) the Bank may issue bank notes for one pound and for ten shillings:

   (b) any such bank notes may be issued at any place out of London without being made payable at that place, and wherever issued shall be payable only at the head office of the Bank:

   (c) any such bank notes may be put into circulation in Scotland and Northern Ireland, and shall be current and legal tender in Scotland and Northern Ireland as in England.

Amendment with respect to powers of Bank of England to issue bank notes

(2) Section six of the Bank of England Act, 1833 (which provides that bank notes shall be legal tender), shall have effect as if for the words "shall be a legal tender to the amount expressed in such note or notes and shall be taken to be valid as a tender to such amount for all sums above five pounds on all occasions on which any tender of money may be

legally made" there were substituted the words "shall be legal tender for the payment of any amount".

(3) The following provisions shall have effect so long as subsection (1) of section one of the Gold Standard Act, 1925, remains in force—

(a) notwithstanding anything in the proviso to section six of the Bank of England Act, 1833, bank notes for one pound or ten shillings shall be deemed a legal tender of payment by the Bank or any branch of the Bank, including payment of bank notes:

(b) the holders of bank notes for five pounds and upwards shall be entitled, on a demand made at any time during office hours at the head office of the Bank or, in the case of notes payable at a branch of the Bank, either at the head office or at that branch, to require in exchange for the said bank notes for five pounds and upwards bank notes for one pound or ten shillings.

(4) The Bank shall have power, on giving not less than three months' notice in the London, Edinburgh and Belfast Gazettes, to call in the bank notes for one pound or ten shillings of any series on exchanging them for bank notes of the same value of a new series.

(5) Notwithstanding anything in section eight of the Truck Act, 1831, the payment of wages in bank notes of one pound or ten shillings shall be valid, whether the workman does or does not consent thereto.

Amount of Bank of England note issue

2. (1) Subject to the provisions of this Act the Bank shall issue bank notes up to the amount representing the gold coin and gold bullion for the time being in the issue department, and shall in addition issue bank notes to the amount of two hundred and sixty million pounds in excess of the amount first mentioned in this section, and the issue of notes which the Bank are by or under this Act required or authorised to make in excess of the said first mentioned amount is in this Act referred to as "the fiduciary note issue".

(2) The Treasury may at any time on being requested by the Bank, direct that the amount of the fiduciary note issue

shall for such period as may be determined by the Treasury, after consultation with the Bank, be reduced by such amount as may be so determined.

3. (1) In addition to the gold coin and bullion for the time being in the issue department, the Bank shall from time to time appropriate to and hold in the issue department securities of an amount in value sufficient to cover the fiduciary note issue for the time being. *Securities for note issue to be held in issue department*

(2) The securities to be held as aforesaid may include silver coin to an amount not exceeding five and one-half million pounds.

(3) The Bank shall from time to time give to the Treasury such information as the Treasury may require with respect to the securities held in the issue department, but shall not be required to include any of the said securities in the account to be taken pursuant to section five of the Bank of England Act, 1819.

4. (1) As from the appointed day all currency notes issued under the Currency and Bank Notes Act, 1914, certified by the Treasury to be outstanding on that date (including currency notes covered by certificates issued to any persons under section two of the Currency and Bank Notes (Amendment) Act, 1914, but not including currency notes called in but not cancelled) shall, for the purpose of the enactments relating to bank notes and the issue thereof (including this Act) be deemed to be bank notes, and the Bank shall be liable in respect thereof accordingly. *Transfer of currency notes issue to Bank of England*

(2) The currency notes to which subsection (1) of this section applies are in this Act referred to as "the transferred currency notes".

(3) At any time after the appointed day, the Bank shall have power, on giving not less than three months' notice in the London, Edinburgh and Belfast Gazettes, to call in the transferred currency notes on exchanging them for bank notes of the same value.

(4) Any currency notes called in but not cancelled before the appointed day may be exchanged for bank notes of the same value.

⟨ 159 ⟩

5. (1) On the appointed day, in consideration of the Bank undertaking liability in respect of the transferred currency notes, all the assets of the Currency Note Redemption Account other than Government securities shall be transferred to the issue department, and there shall also be transferred to the issue department out of the said assets Government securities of such an amount in value as will together with the other assets to be transferred as aforesaid represent in the aggregate the amount of the transferred currency notes.

For the purpose of this subsection the value of any marketable Government securities shall be taken to be their market price as on the appointed day less the accrued interest, if any, included in that price.

(2) Any bank notes transferred to the Bank under this section shall be cancelled.

(3) Such of the said Government securities as are not transferred to the Bank under the foregoing provisions of this section shall be realised and the amount realised shall be paid into the Exchequer at such time and in such manner as the Treasury direct.

6. (1) The Bank shall, at such times and in such manner as may be agreed between the Treasury and the Bank, pay to the Treasury an amount equal to the profits arising in respect of each year in the issue department, including the amount of any bank notes written off under section six of the Bank Act, 1892, as amended by this Act, but less the amount of any bank notes so written off which have been presented for payment during the year and the amount of any currency notes called in but not cancelled before the appointed day which have been so presented.

(2) For the purposes of this section the amount of the profits arising in any year in the issue department shall, subject as aforesaid, be ascertained in such manner as may be agreed between the Bank and Treasury.

(3) For the purposes of the Income Tax Acts, any income of, or attributable to, the issue department shall be deemed to be income of the Exchequer, and any expenses of, or attributable to, the issue department shall be deemed not to be expenses of the Bank.

(4) The Bank shall cease to be liable to make any payment in consideration of their exemption from stamp duty on bank notes.

7. Section six of the Bank Act, 1892 (which authorises the writing off of bank notes which are not presented for payment within forty years of the date of issue), shall have effect as if, in the case of notes for one pound or ten shillings, twenty years were substituted for forty years, and as if, in the case of any such notes being transferred currency notes, they had been issued on the appointed day and, in the case of any such notes not being transferred currency notes, they had been issued on the last day on which notes of the particular series of which they formed part were issued by the Bank. *Amendment of s. 6 of 55 & 56 Vict. c. 48*

8. (1) If the Bank at any time represent to the Treasury that it is expedient that the amount of the fiduciary note issue shall be increased to some specified amount above two hundred and sixty million pounds, the Treasury may authorise the Bank to issue bank notes to such an increased amount, not exceeding the amount specified as aforesaid, and for such period, not exceeding six months, as the Treasury think proper. *Power to increase amount of fiduciary note issue*

(2) Any authority so given may be renewed or varied from time to time on the like representation and in like manner:

Provided that, notwithstanding the foregoing provision, no such authority shall be renewed so as to remain in force (whether with or without variation) after the expiration of a period of two years from the date on which it was originally given, unless Parliament otherwise determines.

(3) Any minute of the Treasury authorising an increase of the fiduciary note issue under this section shall be laid forthwith before both Houses of Parliament.

9. (1) For the purpose of any enactment which in the case of a bank in Scotland or Northern Ireland limits by reference to the amount of gold and silver coin held by any such bank the amount of the notes which that bank may have in circulation, bank notes held by that bank or by the Bank on account of that bank, shall be treated as being gold coin held by that bank. *Amendment as to issue of notes by banks in Scotland and Northern Ireland*

(2) A bank in Scotland or Northern Ireland may hold the coin and bank notes by reference to which the amount of

the bank notes which it is entitled to have in circulation is limited at such of its offices in Scotland or Northern Ireland, respectively, not exceeding two, as may from time to time be approved by the Treasury.

Amendment of s. 6 of 7 & 8 Vict. c. 32

10. The form prescribed by Schedule A to the Bank Charter Act, 1844, for the account to be issued weekly by the Bank under section six of that Act may be modified to such an extent as the Treasury, with the concurrence of the Bank, consider necessary, having regard to the provisions of this Act.

Power of Bank of England to require persons to make returns of and to sell gold

11. (1) With a view to the concentration of the gold reserves and to the securing of economy in the use of gold, the following provisions of this section shall have effect so long as subsection (1) of section one of the Gold Standard Act, 1925, remains in force.

(2) Any person in the United Kingdom owning any gold coin or bullion to an amount exceeding ten thousand pounds in value shall, on being required so to do by notice in writing from the Bank, forthwith furnish to the Bank in writing particulars of the gold coin and bullion owned by that person, and shall, if so required by the Bank, sell to the Bank the whole or any part of the said coin or bullion, other than any part thereof which is bona fide held for immediate export or which is bona fide required for industrial purposes, on payment therefor by the Bank, in the case of coin, of the nominal value thereof, and in the case of bullion, at the rate fixed in section four of the Bank Charter Act, 1844.

Penalty for defacing bank notes

12. If any person prints, or stamps, or by any like means impresses, on any bank note any words, letters or figures, he shall, in respect of each offence, be liable on summary conviction to a penalty not exceeding one pound.

Short title, interpretation and repeal

13. (1) This Act may be cited as the Currency and Bank Notes Act, 1928.

(2) This Act shall come into operation on the appointed day, and the appointed day shall be such day as His Majesty may by Order in Council appoint, and different days may be appointed for different purposes and for different provisions of this Act.

(3) In this Act, unless the context otherwise requires:

The expression "the Bank" means the Bank of England:

The expression "issue department" means the issue department of the Bank:

The expression "bank note" means a note of the Bank:

The expression "coin" means coin which is current and legal tender in the United Kingdom:

The expression "bullion" includes any coin which is not current and legal tender in the United Kingdom.

(4) The enactments set out in the Schedule to this Act are hereby repealed to the extent specified in the third column of that Schedule.

SCHEDULE

ENACTMENTS REPEALED

Session and Chapter	Short Title	Extent of Repeal
7 & 8 Vict. c. 32	The Bank Charter Act, 1844	Sections two, three, five and nine, in section eleven the words from "save and except that" to the end of the section, sections thirteen to twenty, and section twenty-two, and, so far as relates to England, sections ten and twelve
24 & 25 Vict. c. 3	Bank of England Act, 1861	Section four, so far as unrepealed
4 & 5 Geo. 5, c. 14	The Currency and Bank Notes Act, 1914	The whole Act, except subsection (5) of section one and section five
4 & 5 Geo. 5, c. 72	The Currency and Bank Notes (Amendment) Act, 1914	The whole Act
5 & 6 Geo. 5, c. 62	The Finance Act, 1915	Section twenty-seven
15 & 16 Geo. 5, c. 29	The Gold Standard Act, 1925	Paragraph (b) of subsection (1) of section one

APPENDIX C

GOLD STANDARD (AMENDMENT) ACT 1931

An Act to suspend the operation of subsection (2) of section one of the Gold Standard Act, 1925, and for purposes connected therewith. (21 September 1931.)

BE it enacted by the King's most Excellent Majesty, by and with the advice and consent of the Lords Spiritual and Temporal, and Commons, in this present Parliament assembled, and by the authority of the same, as follows:

Suspension of right to purchase gold bullion

1. (1) Unless and until His Majesty by Proclamation otherwise directs, subsection (2) of section one of the Gold Standard Act, 1925, shall cease to have effect, notwithstanding that subsection (1) of the said section remains in force.

(2) The Bank of England are hereby discharged from all liabilities in respect of anything done by the Bank in contravention of the provision of the said subsection (2) at any time after the eighteenth day of September, nineteen hundred and thirty-one, and no proceedings whatsoever shall be instituted against the Bank or any other person in respect of anything so done as aforesaid.

(3) It shall be lawful for the Treasury to make, and from time to time vary, orders authorising the taking of such measures in relation to the exchanges and otherwise as they may consider expedient for meeting difficulties arising in connection with the suspension of the gold standard.

This subsection shall continue in force for a period of six months from the passing of this Act.

Short title

2. This Act may be cited as the Gold Standard (Amendment) Act, 1931.

The Gold Standard (Amendment) Act 1931 states in Section 1 (3):

It shall be lawful for the Treasury to make, and from time to time vary, orders authorising the taking of such measures in relation to the exchanges and otherwise as they may consider expedient for meeting difficulties arising in connection with the suspension of the gold standard. This subsection shall continue in force for a period of six months from the passing of this Act.

With the above as its authority the Treasury issued the following orders:

Order made by the Treasury under Section 1 (3) of the Gold Standard (Amendment) Act, 1931.

The Lords Commissioners of His Majesty's Treasury, in pursuance of Section 1 (3) of the Gold Standard (Amendment) Act, 1931, hereby order that until further notice purchases of foreign exchange, or transfers of funds with the object of acquiring such exchange directly or indirectly, by British Subjects or persons resident in the United Kingdom shall be prohibited except for the purpose of financing

1. Normal trading requirements.
2. Contracts existing before September 21st, 1931.
3. Reasonable travelling or other personal purposes.

PHILIP SNOWDEN.
GEORGE PENNY.
Two of the Lords Commissioners
of the Treasury.

22 September 1931.

Order made by the Treasury under Section 1 (3) of the Gold Standard (Amendment) Act, 1931, varying the Order made by the Treasury under the said Act on the 22 September 1931.

The Lords Commissioners of His Majesty's Treasury, in pursuance of section 1 (3) of the Gold Standard (Amendment) Act 1931, hereby order that the prohibition imposed by the Order made under the said Act by the said Lords Commissioners on the twenty-second day of September, nineteen hundred and thirty-one, shall cease to have effect on the third day of March, nineteen hundred and thirty-two.

N. CHAMBERLAIN.
VICTOR WARRENDER.
Two of the Lords Commissioners
of His Majesty's Treasury.

2 March 1932.

APPENDIX D

FINANCE ACT 1932

Sections 24, 25 and 26

EXCHANGE EQUALISATION ACCOUNT

Establish-
ment of
Exchange
Equalisation
Account

24. (1) There shall be established an account, to be called "the Exchange Equalisation Account", which shall be under the control of the Treasury and shall be used for the purposes specified in this Part of this Act.

(2) The Treasury may, if at any time they think it expedient so to do, cause the Exchange Equalisation Account (in this Part of this Act referred to as "the Account") to be wound up forthwith, and the Account shall in any event be wound up not later than six months after the date on which the Commons House of Parliament resolve that the Account is no longer required for the purpose for which it was established.

(3) The Treasury may cause any funds in the Account to be invested in securities or in the purchase of gold in such manner as they think best adapted for checking undue fluctuations in the exchange value of sterling.

(4) There shall be issued to the Account out of the Consolidated Fund, or the growing produce thereof, at such times and in such manner as the Treasury may direct such sums, not exceeding in the aggregate one hundred and fifty million pounds, as the Treasury may determine, and all the assets of the Exchange Account shall be transferred to the Account at such time as the Treasury may direct.

(5) For the purpose of providing for the issue of sums out of the Consolidated Fund under the last preceding subsection or for the repayment to that Fund of all or any part of any sums so issued, the Treasury may raise money in any manner in which they are authorised to raise money under and for the purposes of subsection (1) of section one of the War Loan Act, 1919, and any securities created and issued to raise money under this subsection shall for all purposes be deemed to have been created and issued under the said subsection (1).

⟨ 166 ⟩

(6) The Bank of England may advance to the Treasury any sums which the Treasury have under this section power to raise.

(7) The Account shall in every year until it is wound up be examined by the Comptroller and Auditor-General in such manner as he, in his discretion, thinks proper with a view to ascertaining whether the operations on and the transactions in connection with the Account have been in accordance with the provisions of this Part of this Act, and he shall certify to the Commons House of Parliament whether in his opinion, having regard to the result of the examination, the operations on and the transactions in connection with the Account have or have not been in accordance with the provisions of this Part of this Act.

25. (1) There shall be paid to the Issue Department of the Bank of England out of the Account such sum not exceeding eight million pounds as is in the opinion of the Treasury equal to the amount of the net loss which by reason of variations in rates of exchange has been sustained in connection with the credits obtained by the Bank of England from the Bank of France and the Federal Reserve Bank of New York on the first day of August, nineteen hundred and thirty-one. *Application of Account, transfers thereto, &c.*

(2) For the purpose of any valuation of the assets held in the Issue Department of the Bank of England, being a valuation made before the winding up of the Account—

(*a*) gold held in the Department shall be taken to be of the value of three pounds seventeen shillings and tenpence halfpenny for every ounce troy of the standard fineness specified in the First Schedule to the Coinage Act, 1870 (hereafter referred to as "the fixed value"); and

(*b*) assets in currencies other than sterling held in the Department shall be valued at the rate of exchange prevailing at the date of each valuation.

(3) Whenever any gold is purchased or sold on account of the Issue Department during the existence of the Account, the amount by which the price of the gold exceeds the fixed value thereof shall, in the case of a purchase, be made good to the Issue Department from the Account, and, in the case of a sale, be made good to the Account from the Issue Department.

(4) Immediately before the Account is wound up, the amount by which the market value (as agreed between the Bank and the Treasury) of the gold then held in the Issue Department exceeds its fixed value shall be made good by the Department to the Account.

(5) If on any sale of assets in currencies other than sterling held in the Issue Department (whether the sale occurred before the establishment of the Account or occurs at any time during the existence of the Account), or on any valuation during the existence of the Account of any such assets, it appears that by reason of variations in rates of exchange occurring at any time after the twenty-first day of September, nineteen hundred and thirty-one, there has been any depreciation or loss in connection with those assets, the amount of the depreciation or loss shall be made good to the Issue Department from the Account, and if on any such sale or valuation as aforesaid it appears that by reason as aforesaid any appreciation or gain has arisen in connection with any of the said assets, the amount of the appreciation or gain shall be made good from the Issue Department to the Account.

(6) Where under this section any amount is to be made good from or to the Account, there may, in lieu of a payment in cash, be transferred from or to the Account securities equivalent in value, in the opinion of the Treasury, to that amount.

(7) It is hereby declared that in subsection (3) of the last preceding section of this Act and in section three of the Currency and Bank Notes Act, 1928 (which relates to the securities to be held in the Issue Department), the expression "securities" includes securities and assets in currency of any country and in whatever form held.

Winding-up of Account 26. On the winding-up of the Account the assets thereof shall be applied in such manner as the Treasury may direct for the redemption of debt, and the Treasury shall thereupon cause to be laid before Parliament a statement of the sum so applied, and of the sums issued out of the Consolidated Fund to the Account, together with a report by the Comptroller and Auditor-General with respect to such matters in relation to the Account as he thinks fit.

N.B. Subsections (2) to (6) of section twenty-five above have been repealed by the Currency and Bank Notes Act 1939, q.v. p. 152.

APPENDIX E

TRIPARTITE CURRENCY AGREEMENT

The following statement was issued by the British Treasury on 26 September 1936:

1. His Majesty's Government, after consultation with the United States Government and the French Government, join with them in affirming a common desire to foster those conditions which will safeguard peace and will best contribute to the restoration of order in international economic relations, and to pursue a policy which will tend to promote prosperity in the world and to improve the standard of living.

2. His Majesty's Government must, of course, in its policy towards international monetary relations, take into full account the requirements of internal prosperity of the countries of the Empire, as corresponding considerations will be taken into account by the Governments of France and of the United States of America.

They welcome this opportunity to reaffirm their purpose to continue the policy which they have pursued in the course of recent years, one constant object of which is to maintain the greatest possible equilibrium in the system of international exchanges and to avoid to the utmost extent the creation of any disturbance of that system by British monetary action. His Majesty's Government share with the Governments of France and the United States the conviction that the continuation of this two-fold policy will serve the general purpose which all Governments should pursue.

3. The French Government inform His Majesty's Government that, judging that the desired stability of the principal currencies cannot be ensured on a solid basis except after the re-establishment of a lasting equilibrium between the various economic systems, they have decided with this object to propose to their Parliament the readjustment of their currency. His Majesty's Government have, as also the United States

Government, welcomed this decision in the hope that it will establish more solid foundations for the stability of international economic relations.

His Majesty's Government, as also the Governments of France and of the United States of America, declare their intention to continue to use the appropriate available resources so as to avoid as far as possible any disturbance of the basis of international exchanges resulting from the proposed readjustment. They will arrange for such consultation for this purpose as may prove necessary with the other two Governments and the authorised agencies.

4. His Majesty's Government are moreover convinced, as are also the Governments of France and the United States of America, that the success of the policy set forth above is linked with the development of international trade. In particular, they attach the greatest importance to action being taken without delay to relax progressively the present system of quotas and exchange controls with a view to their abolition.

5. His Majesty's Government, in common with the Governments of France and the United States of America, desire and invite the co-operation of the other nations to realise the policy laid down in the present declaration.

They trust that no country will attempt to obtain an unreasonable competitive exchange advantage and thereby hamper the effort to restore more stable economic relations which it is the aim of the three Governments to promote.

APPENDIX F

PROTOCOLS TO TRIPARTITE
CURRENCY AGREEMENT

The following statement was issued by the British Treasury on 13 October 1936:

"Arrangements for technical co-operation with the monetary authorities in the United States have now been completed and a new regulation is being published by the Secretary of the Treasury of the United States which will enable gold to be obtained in the United States in exchange for dollars by any country which gives reciprocal facilities to the United States. His Majesty's Government have arranged for such facilities to be afforded in London to the United States authorities. This day-to-day working arrangement should greatly facilitate the technical operations of exchange control; similar arrangements have been made with the Bank of France so as to provide for effective co-operation between the three centres."

The following statement was issued by the British Treasury on 24 November 1936:

"His Majesty's Government have noted with pleasure the declarations of the Governments of the Netherlands and Switzerland, which were issued yesterday, expressing their adherence to the principles stated in the tripartite declaration of 25th September (when the French franc was devalued). The Belgian Government declared their adherence to those principles on 26th September.

"His Majesty's Government are informed that the United States Treasury are extending to Belgium, the Netherlands and Switzerland the arrangements for technical co-operation in exchange matters which were referred to in the statement published on 13th October.

"His Majesty's Government welcome this step, which is in

harmony with the arrangements already made between the United States and this country and between the United States and France.

"The extension of this arrangement is also in harmony with the general basis of mutual co-operation which exists between the British monetary authorities and the Belgian, Netherlands and Swiss monetary authorities."

APPENDIX G

FIGURES RELATING TO INFLUX OF FRENCH CAPITAL 1936

	April			May				June			
	15	22	29	6	13	20	27	3	10	17	24
Gold holding	202·3	202·9	203·5	204·4	205·1	206·1	207·2	208·1	209·4	212·8	217·2
Notes in circulation	421·9	415·4	416·8	422·6	424·7	423·1	426·0	433·4	433·0	432·0	434·7
Estimated net note circulation (average)		402·2			408·7				418·2		
Public Deposits	9·9	13·2	7·4	9·1	13·3	21·0	19·7	8·2	13·4	13·9	20·0
Bankers' Deposits	104·9	93·0	104·7	88·3	83·2	80·0	78·2	89·7	86·5	90·9	90·8
Reserve	40·4	47·4	46·6	41·8	40·3	43·0	41·2	34·7	36·3	40·7	42·4
Proportion %	26·8	36·1	30·8	31·0	30·0	31·2	30·6	25·6	25·5	28·6	28·6
Treasury bill rate (*s. d.*) %	10/7	10/6¾	10/6¼	10/6	10/6	10/6	11/0½	11/5½	14/7	18/1	17/1
Three months' bank bills %	9/16	9/16	9/16	9/16	9/16	9/16	9/16	5/8	3/4	15/16	3/4
(A) Gold increase at statutory price	0·480	0·514	0·590	0·926	0·630	1·072	1·034	0·885	1·215	3·361	4·467
Average market price of gold (*s. d.*)	140/10	140/10¼	140/11	140/7½	140/4¼	140/1¼	139/9	139/2½	138/9¼	138/6½	138/8
(B) Gold increase at market price	0·796	0·852	0·979	1·533	1·041	1·769	1·702	1·451	1·985	5·491	7·296
Difference of (A) and (B)	0·316	0·338	0·389	0·607	0·411	0·697	0·668	0·566	0·770	2·130	2·829
Cumulative difference (borne by E.E.A.)		0·654	1·043	1·650	2·061	2·758	3·426	3·992	4·762	6·892	9·721
Franc-sterling exchange rate	74 15/16	74 15/16	75	75⅜	75 7/16	75 9/16	75⅝	76⅛	76 3/16	76⅝	76⅛

APPENDIX G (*continued*)

	July					August		
	1	8	15	22	29	5	12	19
Gold holding	222·0	226·5	231·9	236·7	240·0	244·0	244·0	244·8
Notes in circulation	439·6	443·0	443·2	445·5	448·5	454·4	450·3	444·5
Estimated net note circulation (average)			426·8				430·2	
Public Deposits	9·9	10·5	20·3	19·9	42·2	17·6	17·4	23·5
Bankers' Deposits	111·7	96·7	90·6	98·2	75·2	92·6	98·0	96·0
Reserve	42·4	43·4	48·6	53·1	52·3	49·5	53·7	60·3
Proportion %	26·3	29·8	32·0	33·9	33·3	33·3	35·0	37·8
Treasury bill rate (*s. d.*) %	12/8	12/1¼	11/9½	11/7½	10/6	10/6½	10/6¼	10/6
Three months' bank bills %	5/8	5/8	5/8	9/16	9/16	9/16	9/16	9/16
(A) Gold increase at statutory price	4·786	4·489	5·394	4·773	4·174	3·019	Nil	0·800
Average market price of gold (*s. d.*)	138/9	139/–	138/10½	138/9¼	138/10	138/8	138/5	138/2
(B) Gold increase at market price	7·821	7·351	8·823	7·800	6·825	4·931	.	1·383
Difference of (A) and (B)	3·035	2·862	3·429	3·027	2·651	1·912	.	0·583
Cumulative difference (borne by E.E.A.)	12·756	15·618	19·047	22·074	24·725	26·637	.	27·200
Franc-sterling exchange rate	75¾	75¾	75⅞	$75\frac{15}{16}$	76	$76\frac{3}{16}$	76⅛	76½

APPENDIX H

DATA COVERING THE EFFLUX OF FRENCH CAPITAL, MAY 1938

BANK OF ENGLAND WEEKLY STATEMENTS 1938 (in £ millions)

	MAY 4	MAY 11	MAY 18	MAY 25	JUNE 1	JUNE 8	JUNE 15	JUNE 22	JUNE 29	JULY 6
NOTES CIRCULATION ...	490·5	482·2	478·6	480·2	484·9	490·7	485·7	483·2	485·2	488·2
GOLD	327·1	327·2	327·1	327·2	327·2	327·3	327·3	327·3	327·3	327·4
PUBLIC DEPOSITS ...	10·7	36·6	28·5	26·5	24·9	11·7	11·6	21·7	10·5	12·5
BANKERS' DEPOSITS ...	117·4	87·9	93·1	91·2	102·8	111·1	109·0	105·5	125·4	115·6
OTHER DEPOSITS ...	35·9	35·4	35·9	36·1	35·4	35·4	25·8	35·3	36·1	35·9
SECURITIES	19·2	27·0	28·5	28·9	28·9	28·1	25·8	26·1	28·4	3·1
GOVERNMENT SECURITIES	117·7	105·7	98·3	95·7	109·7	111·4	111·4	110·2	119·5	111·8
RESERVE	36·7	45·0	48·5	47·0	42·3	37·5	41·5	44·1	42·7	39·1
"PROPORTION" % ...	22·3	28·1	30·7	30·5	25·9	23·0	25·3	27·1	24·4	23·8

FLOATING DEBT*

(in £ millions)

1938	TREASURY BILLS Tender	TREASURY BILLS Tap	WAYS AND MEANS ADVANCES Public Depts.	WAYS AND MEANS ADVANCES Bank of England	TOTAL FLOATING DEBT
APRIL 30	545·0	288·6	36·5	. . .	870·2
MAY 7	560·0	281·6	35·9	8·0	885·4
,, 14	570·0	278·1	39·2	. . .	887·3
,, 21	570·0	276·0	41·8	. . .	887·8
,, 28	570·0	281·4	40·8	. . .	892·2
JUNE 4	575·5	308·7	43·9	2·0	929·6
,, 11	580·0	310·7	41·6	. . .	932·3
,, 18	585·0	303·4	40·1	. . .	928·5
,, 25	583·0	305·7	44·7	. . .	933·4
,, 30	851·0		40·1	. . .	934·0
JULY 9	573·0	298·3	40·1	. . .	914·5

TREASURY BILLS ISSUED BY TENDER*

(in £ millions)

1938	OFFERED	ALLOTTED	AVERAGE RATE % s.	d.
APRIL 29	45·0	45·0	10	1·99
MAY 6	45·0	40·0	10	0·69
,, 13	30·0	30·0	10	1·12
,, 20	35·0	35·0	10	1·11
,, 27	45·0	45·0	10	9·37
JUNE 3	50·0	50·0	12	1·04
,, 10	50·0	50·0	12	9·19
,, 17	50·0	48·0	11	5·68
,, 24	45·0	45·0	10	9·18
JULY 1	45·0	45·0	10	5·33
,, 8	45·0	45·0	10	5·43

* Extracted from the *Economist*.

APPENDIX I

DATA COVERING THE PERIOD OF CRISIS AUGUST–OCTOBER 1938

BANK OF ENGLAND WEEKLY STATEMENTS (in £ millions)

	AUG. 3	AUG. 10	AUG. 17	AUG. 24	AUG. 31	SEPT. 7	SEPT. 14
NOTES CIRCULATION ...	497·8	490·0	482·6	478·7	480·4	480·1	478·6
GOLD	326·4	326·4	326·4	326·4	326·4	326·4	326·4
PUBLIC DEPOSITS ...	9·5	19·3	20·1	24·0	27·8	32·2	21·5
BANKERS' DEPOSITS ...	113·4	106·1	105·7	101·6	94·7	91·3	99·6
OTHER DEPOSITS ...	34·7	34·5	34·1	34·1	36·4	34·8	36·4
SECURITIES	21·8	21·5	22·0	20·6	22·3	22·1	22·1
GOVERNMENT SECURITIES	114·7	109·7	104·6	101·9	102·1	101·3	98·5
RESERVE	29·7	37·6	45·0	48·9	47·3	47·7	49·3
"PROPORTION" % ...	18·8	23·4	28·1	30·6	29·7	30·1	31·2
DOLLAR-STERLING EXCHANGE RATE	4·89½	4·88	4·88⅛	4·88¼	4·85⅛	4·82¼	4·79¾

	SEPT. 21	SEPT. 28	OCT. 5	OCT. 12	OCT. 19	OCT. 26	NOV. 2
NOTES CIRCULATION ...	479·2	500·9	505·8	496·4	486·4	482·5	484·0
GOLD	326·4	326·4	326·4	326·4	326·4	326·4	326·4
PUBLIC DEPOSITS ...	18·4	11·5	12·1	28·3	33·8	25·0	14·1
BANKERS' DEPOSITS ...	100·9	99·9	109·7	94·8	90·9	100·4	109·5
OTHER DEPOSITS ...	39·4	40·2	37·1	36·6	35·8	35·5	36·4
SECURITIES	24·6	22·8	22·5	21·9	23·9	21·6	21·1
GOVERNMENT SECURITIES	97·6	112·8	121·9	114·5	104·9	107·6	102·4
RESERVE	48·7	26·9	22·0	31·4	41·4	45·3	43·8
"PROPORTION" % ...	30·6	17·7	13·8	19·6	25·7	28·1	27·3
DOLLAR-STERLING EXCHANGE RATE	4·82¼	4·61½	4·80	4·74¾	4·77¾	4·77¾	4·75¾

FLOATING DEBT* (in £ millions)

1938	TREASURY BILLS		WAYS AND MEANS ADVANCES		TOTAL FLOATING DEBT
	Tender	Tap	Public Depts.	Bank of England	
AUG. 6	560·0	320·1	44·2	.	924·3
,, 13	555·0	298·4	44·1	.	902·5
,, 20	555·0	296·4	41·9	.	893·1
,, 27	555·0	294·0	45·7	.	894·7
SEPT. 3	550·0	316·9	44·1	.	911·0
,, 10	545·0	324·1	46·0	.	915·1
,, 17	537·0	334·5	48·2	.	919·7
,, 24	526·0	345·5	49·8	.	921·3
,, 30	883·4		49·2	.	932·6
OCT. 8	521·0	379·1	49·3	4·0	953·4
,, 15	526·0	383·6	45·8	.	955·4
,, 22	526·0	379·3	41·4	.	946·7
,, 29	522·0	386·1	44·0	.	952·1
NOV. 5	517·0	405·3	46·1	3·0	971·3

* Extracted from the *Economist*.

APPENDIX I *(continued)*

TREASURY BILLS ISSUED BY TENDER*
(in £ millions)

1938	OFFERED	ALLOTTED	AVERAGE RATE %	
			s.	d.
AUG. 5	35·0	35·0	10	1·80
,, 12	30·0	30·0	10	1·50
,, 19	35·0	35·0	10	1·51
,, 26	40·0	40·0	10	1·53
SEPT. 2	45·0	45·0	10	5·87
,, 9	45·0	42·0	11	11·02
,, 16	40·0	37·0	18	10·75
,, 23	40·0	40·0	19	7·07
,, 30	45·0	45·0	25	1·42
OCT. 7	50·0	50·0	14	3·44
,, 14	50·0	45·0	15	5·57
,, 21	40·0	38·0	13	8·91
,, 28	35·0	35·0	10	9·78
NOV. 4	35·0	35·0	10	5·87

* Extracted from the *Economist*.

APPENDIX K

DEPRECIATION OF PRINCIPAL EUROPEAN CURRENCIES AND OTHERS SINCE SEPTEMBER 1931

(Based on the cost of gold franc 1928)

Pre-war parities
$1·00 = Gold francs 5·1825
$4·866 = £1 = Gold francs 25·2215

Calculated on exchange at 30 June 1938
Pre-war franc. February 1934 dollar
$1·00 = Gold francs 3·061
$4·9543 = £1 = Gold francs 15·1651

	Par prior to 21/9/31	Cost of gold franc 1928	Exchange at 30/6/38	Cost of gold franc 1938	Depreciation %
GREAT BRITAIN	$ 4·8666	£0·0396	$4·9543	£0·0659 =	39·91
BELGIUM	Belgas 35·0000	1·3877	29·2250	1·9271 =	27·99
CZECHO-SLOVAKIA	Kr. 164·2500	6·5123	142·6250	9·4048 =	30·75
DENMARK	Kr. 18·1590	0·7200	22·4000	1·4770 =	51·25
FINLAND	Mks. 193·2300	7·6613	226·7500	14·9520 =	48·76
FRANCE	Frs. 124·2100	4·9248	177·9060	11·7310 =	58·02
GERMANY	Mks. 20·4300	0·8100	12·3000	0·8110 =	0·12
GREECE	Dr. 375·0000	14·8683	547·5000	36·1020 =	58·81
HOLLAND	Fls. 12·1070	0·4800	8·9525	0·5903 =	18·68
ITALY	Lira 92·4600	3·6659	94·1560	6·2087 =	40·95
NORWAY	Kr. 18·1590	0·7200	19·9000	1·3122 =	45·13
POLAND	Zloty 43·3800	1·7200	26·3750	1·7391 =	1·09
PORTUGAL	Esc. 110·0000	4·3614	110·1875	7·2658 =	39·97
ROUMANIA	Lei 813·6000	32·2583	672·5000	44·3450 =	27·25
SPAIN	Ptas. 25·2215	1·0000	150·0000	9·8911 =	89·89
SWEDEN	Kr. 18·1590	0·7200	19·4000	1·2792 =	43·71
SWITZERLAND	Frs. 25·2215	1·0000	21·6150	1·4253 =	29·84
U.S.A.	$ 4·8666	0·1929	4·9543	0·3266 =	40·93

APPENDIX L

DOLLARS TO £

	1931		1932		1933		1934		1935		1936		1937		1938	
	H.	L.	H.	L.	H.	L.	H.	L.	H.	L.	H.	L.	H.	L.	H.	L.
JANUARY	4·85$\frac{41}{64}$	4·85$\frac{5}{16}$	3·49	3·36	3·39$\frac{3}{4}$	3·33$\frac{5}{16}$	5·16	4·95$\frac{1}{4}$	4·94$\frac{3}{8}$	4·84$\frac{1}{4}$	5·00$\frac{1}{2}$	4·92$\frac{13}{16}$	4·91$\frac{3}{8}$	4·89$\frac{3}{4}$	5·01$\frac{3}{16}$	4·99$\frac{1}{8}$
FEBRUARY	4·86$\frac{21}{64}$	4·85$\frac{37}{64}$	3·48$\frac{5}{8}$	3·42$\frac{7}{8}$	3·44$\frac{3}{8}$	3·39$\frac{3}{16}$	5·12$\frac{1}{2}$**d**	4·92**e**	4·88$\frac{7}{8}$	4·85$\frac{3}{4}$	5·02$\frac{3}{4}$	4·98$\frac{3}{8}$	4·90	4·88$\frac{3}{4}$	5·03$\frac{7}{16}$	5·00$\frac{3}{4}$
MARCH	4·86	4·85$\frac{45}{64}$	3·79$\frac{5}{8}$	3·48$\frac{3}{8}$	3·46$\frac{3}{8}$**c**	3·41$\frac{1}{2}$	5·12$\frac{7}{8}$	5·06	4·83$\frac{3}{8}$	4·74$\frac{1}{4}$	4·99$\frac{5}{16}$	4·94$\frac{7}{16}$	4·89	4·87$\frac{27}{32}$	5·01$\frac{7}{8}$	4·95$\frac{1}{2}$
APRIL	4·86$\frac{29}{64}$	4·85$\frac{13}{16}$	3·81$\frac{1}{4}$**b**	3·64$\frac{1}{2}$	3·88	3·41	5·17$\frac{3}{4}$	5·13$\frac{3}{8}$	4·85$\frac{3}{4}$	4·78$\frac{1}{2}$	4·95$\frac{7}{8}$	4·93$\frac{3}{8}$	4·94$\frac{13}{16}$	4·89$\frac{3}{16}$	5·00$\frac{5}{8}$	4·96$\frac{1}{4}$
MAY	4·86$\frac{35}{64}$	4·86$\frac{1}{4}$	3·70	3·65	4·02	3·86$\frac{1}{2}$	5·12$\frac{7}{8}$	5·07	4·95$\frac{5}{8}$	4·82$\frac{1}{2}$	4·99$\frac{3}{4}$	4·93	4·94$\frac{7}{16}$	4·92$\frac{13}{16}$	4·99$\frac{1}{2}$	4·94$\frac{1}{8}$
JUNE	4·86$\frac{45}{64}$	4·86$\frac{17}{64}$	3·69$\frac{3}{8}$	3·60	4·33$\frac{1}{2}$	3·99$\frac{1}{4}$	5·07$\frac{1}{8}$	5·02$\frac{13}{16}$	4·95$\frac{3}{8}$	4·91$\frac{3}{4}$	5·03$\frac{3}{4}$	4·99$\frac{11}{16}$	4·99$\frac{11}{16}$	4·92$\frac{5}{16}$	4·97$\frac{11}{16}$	4·94$\frac{7}{16}$
JULY	4·86$\frac{27}{32}$	4·84$\frac{5}{16}$	3·58$\frac{1}{4}$	3·50	4·84$\frac{5}{8}$	4·30$\frac{1}{4}$	5·06	5·03$\frac{5}{16}$	4·97$\frac{1}{2}$	4·93$\frac{15}{16}$	5·03$\frac{3}{16}$	5·01$\frac{1}{2}$	4·98$\frac{5}{16}$	4·94$\frac{1}{4}$	4·95$\frac{3}{4}$	4·91$\frac{5}{8}$
AUGUST	4·86$\frac{3}{16}$	4·85	3·51$\frac{1}{2}$	3·45$\frac{3}{8}$	4·64$\frac{1}{2}$	4·40$\frac{3}{4}$	5·10$\frac{3}{8}$	4·99$\frac{3}{4}$	4·98$\frac{5}{16}$	4·95$\frac{5}{8}$	5·03$\frac{1}{4}$	5·01$\frac{9}{16}$	4·99$\frac{1}{16}$	4·96$\frac{1}{2}$	4·90$\frac{7}{8}$	4·85$\frac{7}{16}$
SEPTEMBER	4·86$\frac{5}{32}$	3·65**a**	3·49$\frac{1}{4}$	3·45$\frac{1}{8}$	4·83$\frac{3}{8}$	4·52$\frac{5}{8}$	5·01$\frac{13}{16}$	4·96$\frac{1}{4}$	4·95$\frac{7}{8}$	4·91$\frac{3}{16}$	5·07	4·94$\frac{1}{4}$**f**	4·96$\frac{9}{16}$	4·94$\frac{7}{16}$	4·85$\frac{3}{4}$	4·66$\frac{1}{4}$
OCTOBER	3·95$\frac{1}{2}$	3·80	3·45$\frac{5}{8}$	3·27$\frac{5}{8}$	4·79$\frac{1}{4}$	4·48	4·98$\frac{3}{8}$	4·90$\frac{1}{4}$	4·91$\frac{15}{16}$	4·88$\frac{15}{16}$	4·94$\frac{1}{4}$	4·88$\frac{5}{8}$	4·96$\frac{9}{16}$	4·95$\frac{1}{16}$	4·82$\frac{1}{4}$	4·73$\frac{5}{8}$
NOVEMBER	3·81$\frac{1}{4}$	3·45$\frac{1}{4}$	3·33$\frac{1}{2}$	3·17	5·47	4·78$\frac{5}{8}$	5·00$\frac{3}{16}$	4·97$\frac{3}{4}$	4·93$\frac{3}{4}$	4·91$\frac{7}{16}$	4·90$\frac{1}{8}$	4·87$\frac{7}{16}$	5·01$\frac{1}{2}$	4·96$\frac{1}{4}$	4·76	4·63$\frac{3}{8}$
DECEMBER	3·46	3·25$\frac{3}{8}$	3·33$\frac{3}{4}$	3·18$\frac{3}{8}$	5·21$\frac{3}{4}$	5·04$\frac{3}{4}$	4·97$\frac{3}{16}$	4·93$\frac{1}{2}$	4·93$\frac{7}{16}$	4·92$\frac{7}{16}$	4·91$\frac{5}{8}$	4·89$\frac{3}{4}$	5·00$\frac{3}{16}$	4·98$\frac{15}{16}$	4·69$\frac{3}{8}$	4·64$\frac{5}{8}$
FOR YEAR	4·86$\frac{45}{64}$	3·25$\frac{3}{8}$	3·81$\frac{1}{4}$	3·17	5·47	3·33$\frac{5}{16}$	5·17$\frac{3}{4}$	4·90$\frac{1}{4}$	4·98$\frac{5}{16}$	4·74$\frac{1}{4}$	5·07	4·87$\frac{7}{16}$	5·01$\frac{1}{2}$	4·87$\frac{27}{32}$	5·03$\frac{7}{16}$	4·63$\frac{3}{8}$

LONDON–NEW YORK EXCHANGE RATES. Highest and lowest mean daily quotations.

Rates extracted from *Daily Statistic Service*, Exchange Telegraph Co. Ltd.

a *Britain suspended gold standard.*
b *British Exchange Equalisation Account set up.*
c *America suspended gold standard.*
d *America established new gold price.*
e *American Exchange Stabilisation Fund set up.*
f *Tripartite Currency Agreement.*

APPENDIX M

FRENCH FRANCS TO £

	1931		1932		1933		1934		1935		1936		1937		1938	
	H.	L.	H.	L.	H.	L.	H.	L.	H.	L.	H.	L.	H.	L.	H.	L.
JANUARY	123·92a	123·66a	88$\frac{13}{16}$	85$\frac{1}{16}$	87$\frac{1}{16}$	84$\frac{54}{64}$	83$\frac{3}{8}$	79$\frac{13}{32}$	74$\frac{1}{8}$	74$\frac{1}{8}$	75$\frac{6}{64}$	74$\frac{7}{16}$	105$\frac{5}{32}$	105$\frac{9}{64}$	154$\frac{1}{4}$	147$\frac{9}{32}$
FEBRUARY	123·98	123·89	88$\frac{5}{8}$	87$\frac{1}{16}$	88	86$\frac{5}{8}$	79$\frac{7}{8}$	77$\frac{3}{32}$	74$\frac{1}{4}$	73$\frac{1}{16}$	75$\frac{5}{64}$	74$\frac{3}{32}$	105$\frac{5}{32}$	105	154$\frac{5}{32}$	151$\frac{1}{4}$
MARCH	124·22½	123·97½	96$\frac{1}{16}$	88$\frac{5}{16}$	88$\frac{3}{32}$	86$\frac{7}{16}$	77$\frac{1}{16}$	77	73$\frac{1}{2}$	71$\frac{1}{16}$	75$\frac{3}{32}$	74$\frac{21}{64}$	107$\frac{7}{8}$	105$\frac{1}{2}$	164$\frac{3}{4}$	153$\frac{7}{16}$
APRIL	124·43½	124·17	96$\frac{27}{32}$	92$\frac{1}{2}$	89$\frac{7}{16}$	86$\frac{5}{32}$	78$\frac{1}{8}$	77$\frac{3}{32}$	73$\frac{21}{32}$	72$\frac{19}{32}$	75$\frac{1}{16}$	74$\frac{6}{64}$	111$\frac{11}{32}$	106$\frac{11}{32}$	165$\frac{1}{2}$	158$\frac{1}{2}$
MAY	124·45½	124·16½	93$\frac{11}{16}$	92$\frac{1}{2}$	86$\frac{1}{4}$	84$\frac{3}{8}$	77$\frac{3}{32}$	76$\frac{21}{32}$	75$\frac{1}{16}$	73	75$\frac{1}{16}$	75$\frac{6}{64}$	110$\frac{1}{16}$	109$\frac{1}{2}$	178$\frac{1}{2}$c	163$\frac{1}{2}$c
JUNE	124·28½	124·11	93$\frac{1}{16}$	91$\frac{11}{16}$	86$\frac{19}{32}$	85$\frac{1}{16}$	77	76$\frac{9}{32}$	75$\frac{1}{8}$	74$\frac{9}{32}$	76$\frac{1}{8}$	75$\frac{6}{64}$	110$\frac{1}{16}$	110$\frac{1}{4}$	178$\frac{1}{2}$	177$\frac{19}{32}$
JULY	124·28½	123·12½	91$\frac{3}{16}$	89$\frac{9}{16}$	86$\frac{3}{16}$	84$\frac{21}{32}$	76$\frac{3}{4}$	76$\frac{1}{16}$	75$\frac{1}{8}$	74$\frac{1}{16}$	76$\frac{7}{16}$	75$\frac{1}{16}$	134$\frac{1}{16}$	124$\frac{3}{4}$	178$\frac{1}{4}$	177$\frac{1}{8}$
AUGUST	123·97	123·62½	89$\frac{9}{32}$	88$\frac{1}{16}$	85	81$\frac{13}{16}$	76$\frac{13}{32}$	74$\frac{1}{16}$	75$\frac{5}{32}$	74$\frac{3}{4}$	76$\frac{7}{8}$	76$\frac{1}{8}$	132$\frac{9}{32}$	132$\frac{5}{32}$	178$\frac{7}{8}$	178$\frac{5}{16}$
SEPTEMBER	123·95	91·00	89$\frac{7}{16}$	88$\frac{1}{8}$	82$\frac{7}{16}$	79	75$\frac{5}{32}$	74$\frac{7}{8}$	75$\frac{5}{32}$	74$\frac{13}{32}$	77	76$\frac{5}{64}$	146$\frac{5}{8}$	132$\frac{25}{32}$	179$\frac{3}{4}$	178$\frac{5}{16}$
OCTOBER	100·37	96·50	88$\frac{1}{4}$	83$\frac{13}{32}$	82$\frac{9}{16}$	78$\frac{1}{4}$	75$\frac{9}{32}$	73$\frac{7}{8}$	74$\frac{3}{4}$	74$\frac{1}{8}$	105$\frac{13}{32}$b	104$\frac{13}{16}$b	150$\frac{1}{4}$	146$\frac{1}{4}$	179$\frac{1}{16}$	178$\frac{5}{8}$
NOVEMBER	91·81	88·31	85$\frac{1}{8}$	81$\frac{1}{4}$	84$\frac{7}{16}$	79$\frac{1}{4}$	76$\frac{1}{32}$	75$\frac{13}{32}$	75$\frac{5}{64}$	74$\frac{3}{32}$	105$\frac{3}{8}$	105$\frac{1}{8}$	147$\frac{1}{16}$	147$\frac{1}{16}$	178$\frac{7}{8}$	178$\frac{3}{8}$
DECEMBER	88·12	83·12	85$\frac{1}{2}$	81$\frac{15}{16}$	84$\frac{1}{2}$	83$\frac{1}{4}$	75$\frac{16}{32}$	74$\frac{21}{32}$	74$\frac{15}{32}$	74$\frac{13}{32}$	105$\frac{5}{32}$	105$\frac{9}{64}$	147$\frac{9}{32}$	147$\frac{3}{32}$	178$\frac{1}{4}$	176$\frac{5}{8}$
FOR YEAR	124·45½	83·12	96$\frac{27}{32}$	81$\frac{1}{16}$	89$\frac{3}{16}$	78$\frac{1}{2}$	83$\frac{3}{8}$	73$\frac{3}{8}$	75$\frac{1}{16}$	71$\frac{1}{16}$	105$\frac{13}{32}$	74$\frac{1}{16}$	150$\frac{1}{2}$	105	179$\frac{1}{8}$	147$\frac{9}{32}$

LONDON–PARIS EXCHANGE RATES. Highest and lowest mean daily quotations

Rates extracted from *Daily Statistic Service, Exchange Telegraph Co. Ltd.*

a *Poincaré franc.*   b *Auriol franc (Tripartite Currency Agreement).*   c *Daladier franc.*

GLOSSARY

As the meaning of many technical terms used in this work may not be apparent in the text, definitions of the most important are given below:

EXCHANGE EQUALISATION ACCOUNT

"It is a small Government Department, supplied with a predetermined amount of Treasury Bills which it can sell to acquire sterling. This sterling is then sold to holders of foreign currencies, with the result that the Account has changed part of its assets from Treasury Bills into foreign currencies. The rate at which the foreign exchange is acquired is determined by the Account, and by adjusting the rate it can influence the speed at which its Treasury Bills are turned into foreign exchange and vice versa." Professor N. F. Hall, *Exchange Equalisation Account*.

OFFSETTING

"The acquisition of gold and foreign exchange without a corresponding increase in the credit structure." Professor N. F. Hall, *Exchange Equalisation Account*.

And the converse—the relinquishing of gold and foreign exchange without a corresponding decrease in the credit structure.

OPEN-MARKET OPERATIONS

This term refers to operations undertaken by the Bank of England when it wishes to contract or expand the credit base of the banking system. When it wishes to contract credit it will sell securities and by so doing will reduce the cash in the market. When it wishes to expand credit it will buy securities and in so doing places additional cash in the market. Before 1931 open-market operations were often undertaken as an alternative to a change in Bank Rate or to make Bank Rate effective when changed. Since the E.E.A. was established, the open-market policy has been used to control the cash supply irrespective of Bank Rate, and often to reinforce the operations of the E.E.A. (See p. 38.)

Central Bank

"By a Central Bank is meant an institution upon which has been conferred, by law or custom, the responsibility for the smooth running of the credit and/or currency system of a particular area." Professor T. E. Gregory.

Consolidated Fund

"The Consolidated Fund of the United Kingdom is the Fund into which is paid the whole of the revenue, and out of which payments are made, as provided by Parliament." *Dictionary of Banking*.

Funded Debt

"A debt which is permanent, like Consols; that is, a debt upon which the Government pays regular interest without being under any obligation to repay the principal." *Dictionary of Banking*.

Unfunded Debt

"Consists mainly of Treasury Bills, Ways and Means advances, Exchequer Bonds, War Stock and Bonds, National Savings Certificates." *Dictionary of Banking*.

Floating Debt

"For practical purposes the term 'floating debt' may be regarded as synonymous with the amount of Treasury Bills outstanding, for the other component of floating debt, ways and means advances, is at all times comparatively small." *Midland Bank Monthly Review*, July–August 1937.

Short-loan Fund

"By this is meant the money in the hands of the Bank of England and other London banks available for granting loans to bill-brokers, stockbrokers and others for short periods of a few days. In ordinary times this floating capital does not vary much in total amount, but it is constantly varying in position, the rate of interest charged being lowest when almost the whole sum is in the hands of the competing banks and highest when the Bank of England controls a large part of it. The loans made by the Bank to bill-brokers out of this so-called fund are for fixed periods of from three to ten days and at one half per cent above Bank rate. It will easily be understood that the brokers endeavour to get the money they require from the

⟨ 183 ⟩

outside banks first, partly on account of the more moderate rate of interest and partly because they will be able to arrange loans which are not fixed but can be paid off in a day or two, if it suits the convenience of the borrower." *Dictionary of Banking.*

TREASURY BILLS

"These bills are issued by the Treasury under 40 Vict. c. 2, for money borrowed by the Government and form part of the unfunded debt of the country. They may be payable at three, six or nine, but not more than twelve months from the date of the bill. The principal money of any Treasury Bill is charged on and payable out of the Consolidated Fund of the United Kingdom. They are issued by the Bank of England under authority of a warrant from the Treasury. It is said that Treasury Bills were invented by Mr Walter Bagehot in 1877. They carry no interest but are tendered for at a discount." *Dictionary of Banking.*

There are two kinds of Treasury Bills—tender and tap. "These last are placed by the Treasury with the 'public departments' including the Exchange Equalisation Account, the National Debt Commissioners—the body responsible for the placing of large sums on behalf of public or semi-public funds and institutions—and the office of the Paymaster-General." *Midland Bank Monthly Review,* July–August 1937.

Tender Treasury Bills are issued each week in previously determined amounts and are tendered for by banks, discount houses, other business undertakings and Members of Parliament. The bills are allotted pro rata to the highest bidders who, of course, are placed in competition with one another.

Treasury Bills represent the cheapest form of borrowing. For the banks they are assets of the highest order, easily liquidated and therefore form a reserve second only to cash.

GOLD STANDARD

The term "Gold Standard" is generally understood to mean a system of currency, the backing for which is gold, but in point of fact there are at least three different types of gold standard. They are:

(1) Gold Specie Standard

This type of gold standard was operated by Britain before 1914. Gold coins were in circulation and the currency notes were Bank of England notes, the smallest denomination being for £5. These notes were payable on demand in gold. In addition the Bank of England was obliged by the Bank Charter Act 1844 to buy gold offered to it at a price of 77s. 9d. per standard ounce.

(2) Gold Bullion Standard

This type of gold standard was operated by Britain from 1819 to 1821. The Act of 2 July 1819 required the Bank of England to pay its notes in gold bars of a minimum weight of 60 ounces each, at rates per standard ounce which were to rise by graduated stages to 77s. 10½d. per ounce by not later than 1 May 1821. A gold bullion standard was again operated by Britain from 1925 to 1931. The Gold Standard Act 1925 suspended the issue of gold coin and also the convertibility of currency notes to gold at face value. It placed upon the Bank of England the obligation to sell gold bullion to any person who paid the purchase price of 77s. 10½d. per standard ounce, but only in the form of bars containing approximately four hundred ounces troy of fine gold. The Currency and Bank Notes Act 1928 required all persons in possession of gold coin or bullion exceeding ten thousand pounds in value to give notice of the fact in writing to the Bank of England and if requested to do so to sell to the Bank the whole or any part of the gold coin or bullion so held, unless required for export or industrial purposes, at the price fixed by the Bank Charter Act. The obligation to sell gold bullion contained in Clause 2 of the Gold Standard Act 1925 was suspended on 21 September 1931 by the Gold Standard (Amendment) Act 1931.

(3) Gold Exchange Standard

"Under this standard the authority concerned is charged with the duty of keeping the currency at a parity with gold by the indirect method of buying and selling exchange on countries working on a full gold standard. Hence, if the currency becomes too dear in terms of gold the authorities sell it in a gold standard centre. If it becomes too cheap the authorities buy it. To do so they must have control of some reserve of gold standard currencies, or the means to borrow them." H. C. F. Holgate, *Foreign Exchange*.

In 1898 the Indian Government established a gold exchange standard and made its currency convertible into English currency. By maintaining balances in London it could withdraw gold on demand from the Bank of England.

After the Gold Standard Act 1925 many countries maintained a gold exchange standard with sterling as the currency. After the suspension in 1931 many of them continued to base their currency system on sterling. Many more have since joined the sterling "club", and all those countries may be said to operate to "sterling exchange standard".

MANAGED CURRENCY SYSTEM

The currency systems of this country for 150 years have been "managed" systems, more or less. Even when gold bullion or gold specie standards have been operated, each of which was primarily automatic in its working, there was in addition a certain amount of conscious control of the credit supply. Managed currency systems, like open-market operations, as means to an end, are not new; they date back to the end of the eighteenth century. The modern meaning of a "managed currency system" is one that has nothing of the automaticity of a gold standard and one in which the currency is inconvertible paper. The supply of notes in issue and the credit available is not regulated by the gold held by the Bank of England but by the will of Parliament, carried out by the Treasury and the Bank of England.

EARMARKING

Gold held by one Central Bank may be sold to another. In order to save the expenses that would be incurred by transporting the gold to the buyer the Central Bank selling the gold may be asked to hold the amount in its vaults for the account of the buyer. It is then said to be "earmarked".

DOLLAR SHIPPING PARITY. (See pp. 88–97.)

Sometimes referred to as the "American Shipping Parity". "The American Shipping Parity is the price for gold in the London market at which it would be profitable to ship gold to New York, taking into account the ruling sterling-dollar rate." Bank for International Settlements' *Annual Report*, 1938.

"PREMIUM" and "DISCOUNT" in the sterling gold price. (See pp. 88–97.)

⟨ 186 ⟩

INFLATION

"An increase of currency beyond the amount necessary to supply the needs of trade at the existing level of prices." Professor J. H. Jones, *The Economics of Private Enterprise*.

An inflationary condition is said to exist when the banking system's cash basis is increased by artificial means.

DEFLATION

The reverse of inflation. A deflationary condition is said to exist when the banking system is deprived of some part of its cash by artificial means.

REFLATION

Sometimes used synonymously with inflation. More correctly it means the adjustment which is applied when deflation has been carried too far.

INDEX

⟨ 189 ⟩